Ancient Peoples and Places

THE ORIGINS
OF ROME

General Editor

DR. GLYN DANIEL

Ancient Peoples and Places

THE ORIGINS OF ROME

Raymond Bloch

60 PHOTOGRAPHS
17 LINE DRAWINGS
AND 5 MAPS

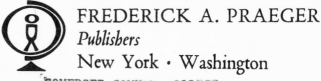

FREDERICK A. PRAEGER
Publishers
New York · Washington

THIS IS VOLUME FIFTEEN IN THE SERIES

Ancient Peoples and Places

GENERAL EDITOR: DR.GLYN DANIEL

BOOKS THAT MATTER *Published in the United States of America*
in 1960 by Frederick A. Praeger, Inc.
Publishers, 111 Fourth Avenue
New York 3, N.Y.
Third printing, 1966
All rights reserved
Library of Congress Catalog Card Number: 60-8075
© Thames and Hudson London 1960
Printed in Great Britain by Wood Westworth & Co. Ltd.
St. Helens, Lancashire

CONTENTS

CONTENTS

ILLUSTRATIONS

Introduction

THE SUBJECT OF ROME'S ORIGINS has never ceased to interest scholars and men of culture. The Ancients themselves felt great sympathetic curiosity about the founding and early progress of a city which, for the first time in the history of the world, united the whole of the West. Numerous passages in Latin literature speak of the coming of the heroes or the time when the Latin and Sabine shepherds settled on the Tiberine hills and many important works of widely differing kinds are entirely devoted to these themes: the second book of Cicero's *De Republica,* all the beginning of Livy's *History* and the whole of Virgil's epic immediately spring to mind. The Roman imagination continued to preserve a very clear and vital image of the beginnings of the *Urbs,* and the same is true of later generations and peoples. Figures like Aeneas and Romulus have kept a place of their own in European consciousness and exerted an extraordinary influence on poets and historians through the ages.

Today the birth of Rome is once again a focus of extremely lively interest, not to say ardent and fruitful controversy. Recent advances in our knowledge have made possible a new understanding of the Ancients' traditions and legendary accounts regarding the founding of Rome and a more precise analysis of the exact conditions of its actual founding. My earlier book in this series dealt with the history of the Etruscan people, whose military and economic expansion was over-whelming and who almost succeeded in unifying the whole peninsula, to their own advantage, before ever Rome's great career began. This book deals with the knotty problem of the beginnings of Rome itself—a city whose patience and tenacity overcame hardships which had vanquished the Etruscans—a richer, more brilliant people, but less dogged and able in matters of political organization.

The subject is a large one and its many separate themes are considered in turn. Slow but sure, history continues to make progress in its attempt to achieve a faithful reconstruction of the past. Owing to the large and increasing number of studies concerning the archaeology and legends of primitive Rome it is possible today to form a much more exact idea of Roman life in its first centuries than was possible, say, a hundred years ago. Even so, such a synthesis may, of course, be considered premature when so many lines of research are still incomplete. Nevertheless, the historian can assess the value of the documentation available to date; he can discuss the problems and so give a clearer picture of the subject. Few subjects deserve this work more than the early, formative period of Roman history.

CHAPTER I

Current Ideas and New Theories

FOR THE PURPOSE of this book it is essential to start by outlining the current position of the scholarly world with regard to the birth and beginnings of Rome. It is particularly important because the attitude of today differs widely not only from that of the Ancients themselves, but also from the views which, until recently, were held by modern scholars. An account of a few recently formulated methodological principles will set the new picture for those readers who may unconsciously retain the broad outlines of the classical accounts, such as Gibbon's *Decline and Fall of the Roman Empire* or Montesquieu's justly famed *Considérations sur la Grandeur et la Décadence des Romains*, on which the conventional classical education is based. But it is not only dated essays of this kind which have been superseded; modern research is equally opposed to the hypercritical positions adopted at the beginning of this century towards the myths and legends surrounding the emergence of the *Urbs*. Nowadays the tendency, a justifiable one, is to discover in these a historical basis.

It is impossible to over-emphasize the broadening of outlook which has modified and enriched our picture of the first centuries. Until recently—and even today, in popular opinion—the birth and development of archaic Rome were seen as, in some way, unique phenomena, absolute realities which could be sufficiently explained by geographical and ethnic conditions and intrinsic necessities. According to this view, Rome evolved from her semi-legendary beginnings, more or less autonomously, into the power that was to conquer first the Italian peninsula and then the whole Mediterranean basin.

This was, in fact, a survival of the traditional narrow outlook of the Roman historians whose starting-point was always the amazing destiny of Republican and Imperial Rome, and who were therefore unable to set the city's beginnings in the context of wider realities of which they knew little or nothing. Continuity, internal coherence, a direct progression to the height of power, then uninterrupted, quasi-fatal, decadence—these were the components of the traditional picture, based firmly on stories from classical literature. It seemed, moreover—but only seemed—to be supported by archaeological evidence.

The progress made by research, both archaeological and linguistic, has shown that this picture bore little relationship to reality. The first civilization to which the name of Latin can be applied, the first occupation of the site of Rome, took place during a century remarkable for cultural achievements of the first importance throughout Italy. It was, in fact, during the Early Iron Age that Italy began to reduce the enormous gap between her own cultural progress and that of the Eastern Mediterranean. A whole outcrop of different cultures had appeared throughout the peninsula from north to south, and what was happening in Latium cannot be understood without an appreciation of the evolution that was taking place in other provinces. Moreover, within this vast movement, of capital importance for Italian protohistory, two higher cultures emerged which were to have a profound effect on the future histories of neighbouring countries; these were the Etruscan culture in Tuscany and, with the arrival of the first Greek colonists, the Hellenic culture on the coasts of Campania, Bruttium, Lucania and Sicily. Now, Latium was exactly in the middle of these two expansion-areas without which the history of Italy would have been quite different. Consequently, from a very early date the influence of Greece on the one hand and Etruria on the other—the latter in itself open to Greek influences, which invaded various fields of its public and private life—was very marked.

But we can go still further. As our archaeological and other documentation increases, it becomes increasingly clear that from the eighth to the fifth century B.C. (i.e. the period corre- sponding with the legendary Roman monarchy) there existed an archaic Tyrrhenian world which unified the course of history in the western half of Central Italy. Apart from certain regional differences which must not, of course, be ignored, this archaic world, comprising Etruria, Latium and Campania, constituted a historic reality which became more and more precisely defined and in which Rome played an important part. In other words, during the first centuries of her existence Rome was part of a large and important cultural zone which explains many aspects of her character and evolution. Various significant social, political and military events from her archaic history become explicable once they are placed against the background of the Tyrrhenian world. If proof of this is needed, take the fact that it was thought for a long time, on the strength of what Roman historians had written, that the decline of the monarchy and the emergence of the Republic were purely Roman phenomena, stemming from internal politics. Today it is known that this political crisis at the end of the sixth century B.C. was far from being an isolated case. The whole of Central Italy experienced something similar, and many cities underwent comparable crises. The decline of the *rex* or *lucumon* led to different solutions in different places. But almost everywhere hierarchic, collegiate magistratures took the place of the fallen monarchies. In many Etruscan cities, as in Rome, a Patrician state developed after the expulsion of the kings and all essential power fell into the hands of an oligarchy of *principes*.

In the ensuing pages many further illustrations of these two approaches will be given; the clearest and most convincing are those concerning the period of the Etruscan kings in Rome. It is true to say that the historical climate of Tarquinian Rome can be better understood by studying the Apollo of Veii, the scenes of social and domestic life on the Tarquinian Tomb of the Baron, the poetry of Ibycus of Rhegium or Simonides of Ceos, the fragments of Hecataeus of Miletus or the character of the great Pythagoras, who gave so much to both Greeks and Tyrrhenians, than by inquiring, however painstakingly, into the deeds and words of the Roman kings as recounted by history, clothed as they are in neo-classical dress, in the manner of the annalists.

Already the half-legendary, half-historical phase of Rome's primitive history has taken on a new appearance. The picture is now illumined by the complex relationships between the City and its neighbours in Latium, the Osco-Umbrian peoples and, above all, the Etrusco-Greek culture, whose fruitful influence cannot be over-emphasized. Before turning to the tribes settled on the Tiberine heights, therefore, it will be useful to sketch an outline of the various peoples who were living in the different regions of the peninsula at the beginning of the Early Iron Age, and to describe the essential features, at least, of their cultures.

The new approach continues to envisage Italy as divided into two by the long, complex Apennine range; this is permissible, for the massif crossing the peninsula as it does, from north to south, isolates the two halves in a way which explains to a certain extent the distinctions between different regions. Moreover, with the exception of the Po, which crosses the great fertile plain in the north from west to east, all the rivers are of the Mediterranean type and are, consequently, rarely navigable. However, the roads following these waterways served to link up regions separated by mountain barriers, and present-day archaeological opinion inclines to the view that, from proto-historic times, cultural trends and influences were transmitted along the valleys and usable routes (still followed by modern roads and railways). Then there was the long-drawn-out Italian coastline, bordering both the Tyrrhenian and the Adriatic Sea. Boats too were an important form of communication, even when they were confined to coastal traffic. Finally, Rome was near Sabine country, Etruria and even Campania, all of which were conveniently situated for cultural and economic exchanges.

Another point that must be clarified at the outset concerns the attitude which should be adopted towards the wealth of Greek and Latin writings dating from the end of the Republic and the beginning of the Empire, which claim to describe the founding of Rome. Numerous generations of schoolchildren in England and elsewhere have been brought up on these accounts, which have become an integral part of their cultural heritage. The question of their historical value was not raised until the eighteenth century. Gradually, as historical methods developed, people began to question how much fact could survive in a tradition which had been handed down orally through the centuries and which might therefore be suspected of alterations if not of complete perversions. Latin epigraphy remained very scant and undeveloped until the last centuries of the Republic. Similarly, the yearly calendar established by the priests, which indicated the magistracies, feasts and main events of each year, was jealously guarded by them; and it was not until the third century B.C., probably 296, when plebeians were admitted to the pontificate, that it was exhibited to the general public by being published and stuck on the *Tabula Pontificis*. Consequently the Roman annalists had living proofs at their disposal only for the period following this date.

As early as the eighteenth century a Frenchman, Louis de Beaufort, wrote a work with the significant title *De l'incertitude des cinq premiers siècles de Rome*, and historical criticism, gradually crystallizing its aims and methods, discovered a fruitful field for research in the highly coloured accounts of the Roman annalists. The severity of the criticism naturally varied from period to period and from critic to critic. It reached its climax at the beginning of the present century with the attitude of men like Pais and his disciples. Pais, pushing destructive analysis to

17

the point of hypercriticism on principle, refused outright to accept a tradition which he saw as saturated with falsehood and fiction.

The modern view is quite different. It is true that the psycho-logical make-up of Greek and Latin authors made them warp reality when dealing with the origins of Rome, and this basic fact was pointed out at the very beginning of this book. These authors were considering a Rome which had already become the political and military centre of Italy and the Mediterranean world, and everything in the history they were writing seemed to lead up to the power and greatness of their own period. Contemporaries of Sulla, Caesar or Augustus could not imagine a Roman past during which for centuries Rome was attached by complex links to towns and regions which gave her a lead in culture and progress. They could not conceive of a world governed by ideals and interests completely different from their own. The false picture of a self-sufficient Rome, working out a destiny peculiar to herself from the beginning, is a direct consequence of this psychological factor.

But this admission does not automatically imply complete scepticism. Many other literatures have shown how faithfully oral traditions could be handed down from generation to generation, and in every sphere of ancient history modern research is revealing the solid core of historical reality which lies behind legendary traditions. With regard to the origins of Rome, the archaeological excavations now taking place on the site give ample confirmation of the truth of many of the tradi-tional views. Numerous examples will be given in the chapters that follow. At this stage it is enough to mention only the most striking and incontrovertible. The well-known legend dates the foundation of Rome by Romulus to the middle of the eighth century B.C., and this date forms the starting-point of all the Roman historians' complex accounts. Today, thanks to pottery found on the spot, excavations have been able to show that the oldest layer, corresponding to the first occupation of the site, belongs to about this date. In other words, Roman memories remained accurate as to this important point; a fact which gives cause for reflection and casts doubt on the cogency of over-severe criticism of ancient historiography.

The same applies to the traditional description of the power of Etruscan Rome under the Tarquins. Excavations have amply confirmed the picture painted by Livy on the authority of the annalists used in his *Histories*. Finds such as the monu- Plates 43–7, 50, 51
mental base of the temple of the Capitoline triad and the varied ornamentation of its many sanctuaries support the theory *Figs. 16, 17*
of a prosperous sixth-century Rome. *Bucchero* and Attic vases, the antefixes of Sant' Omobono and the Etruscan inscriptions discovered at the foot of the Capitol and the Palatine Hill suggest that Etruscan Rome was not unlike the 'lucumonies' of southern Etruria. This is a far cry from the sweeping negativity of Pais, who relegated all traditions regarding Rome before the fourth century to the status of fables. On the contrary, archae- ology strikingly confirms the accuracy of many of them, whether they deal with the topographical development of the city at about 500 B.C., its wealth and splendour, its artistic pro- ductions, or the actual presence of the Etruscans in a position of leadership.

It is clear, therefore, that, though the annalists' outlook led them unconsciously to twist reality, it did not cause the essential dates or facts about the culture of early Rome to be completely forgotten. It is true that the traditional history of the beginnings of the Republic involved still more sources of error, above all anachronisms and conscious distortions stemming from the desire of one famous *gens* or another to date its fame from the very beginning of the new régime. But despite all this confusion, certain precise facts survived, for example, those concerning the foundation of new temples and the introduction of new cults on Roman soil. The religious historian has at his disposal a series of landmarks by means of which he can follow the whole evolution of the religion of the *Urbs* step by step.

The methodological position of the present-day scholar is now clear. The accepted facts of ancient tradition must, of course, be carefully, even ruthlessly, sifted, but it is not necessary to be convinced *a priori* of the inaccuracy of the annalistic account, unless forgery or perversion have been proved. Frequently a close analysis shows that behind the warped account lies a solid basis of fact. Thus rejection of tradition becomes a possible conclusion rather than an inevitable premise. In fact, a considerable portion of tradition has now passed from the sphere of legend into that of history.

CHAPTER II

Peoples and Civilizations of Prehistoric Italy

IT IS IMPOSSIBLE to deal with all the questions, often both difficult and complex, raised by Italian pre, and proto, history. Merely to list the articles and books dealing with these controversial themes would take a whole volume in itself. In any case, many of these problems are still debatable and obscure. But the early days of Latium and Rome herself cannot be understood without a knowledge of the ethnic and cultural picture presented by Italy at the beginning of the first millen, nium B.C. Indeed the Latins were only one of a large number of peoples of different origin and make,up, and the relations of Rome, close or otherwise, with them help to illuminate her own history. We will confine ourselves here to a brief considera, tion of the most important question.[1]

Italy was slow in entering the field of progress in the third and second millennia B.C. There had been nothing to corre, spond with the brilliant cultures of the Eastern Mediterranean. However, during the Neolithic and Bronze Ages ways of life and cultures developed which are worth alluding to, for the ultimate origin of the Italic peoples dates back to those distant periods. Roughly at the beginning of the second millennium B.C., the so,called Eneolithic cultures were already having a certain success. Remains of hut,villages and rock,tombs, yielding abundant and homogeneous material, have been found over the whole peninsula. Recent excavations, following sound stratigraphic methods, have greatly extended our knowledge of the relations between eastern and western civilizations. And careful research in Liguria and in the Lipari islands has thrown light on the extent of, and the various vicissitudes suffered by,

---

[1] The bibliography at the end of this book lists works which consider the various controversies and lines of research in detail.

Fig. 3

the trade that united Italy and Sicily with the Aegean world, from the first half of the second millennium B.C. onwards.

In the linguistic sphere there was an important occurrence in the Bronze Age during the second millennium. A new linguis-tic family, now called Indo-European, developed and soon imposed itself on the previous one (Mediterranean or pre-Indo-European), of which only a few vestiges remain in place-names. This important step in Italian protohistory poses several difficult problems: when did it take place, why and how did it come about, what is the link between the linguistic phenomenon and the supposed ethnic changes? Pigorini's long-popular hypo-thesis that there was a movement coming from the north and sweeping southwards seems to have been exploded by the rival theory of a movement from east to west across the Adriatic. It is still extremely difficult to reconcile, even partially, the linguis-tic phenomena of this remote period with the cultural phases indicated by archaeology. In itself the theory postulated by Pigorini and W. Helbig appeared coherent and systematic; it suggested that tribes moving south through the Alpine passes brought with them the Indo-European languages, settled in the Po valley, in *terramare*, the villages characteristic of the Bronze Age, and bestowed on Italy their languages and customs, the most important of which was the funerary rite of cremation.

But that there is necessarily any connexion between ethnic change on the one hand and language and culture on the other, is questionable. The current view is summed up in V. Gordon Childe's words: 'Culture and race do not coincide.' Various multiple and complex trends and influences, dating from the protohistoric age, could have been just as instrumental in the diffusion of new languages and cultures as ethnic movements and actual folk-migrations. Consequently language, culture and race are no longer inevitably linked together. The views of today are more subtle, less dogmatic.

Even from the archaeological point of view, the Bronze Age,

during which the Indo-Europeanization of the peninsula began, is neither as simple nor as uniform as was long supposed. Scholars such as Rellini, Patroni and others have proved the existence of two quite distinct cultural movements. The first is represented by the *terramare*, the curious villages composed of pile-dwellings surrounded by a protective ditch. Their sites have yielded numerous examples of a species of black, glossy pottery and bronze weapons. But this culture is only a regional phenomenon: there is evidence of it only in the north, especially in Emilia; it is certainly not as fundamentally important as Pigorini and his followers imagined. Along the Apennine range there was another type of culture commonly called Apennine. The excavations of the last twenty years have uncovered more and more traces of it; one need only visit the Pigorini Prehistoric Museum at Rome or the new National Museum of the Marches at Ancona to see and admire the wealth and variety of its material. A book published in 1959[1] summed up the results of recent researches. These have revealed hut-villages and cemeteries in which the rite of inhumation was practised; the material found includes many bronze objects and a form of pottery in black *impasto* with incised decoration. An important vase-form developed, the biconical amphora. In several parts of Italy, as for instance in the Tyrrhenian islands of Lipari and Ischia, traces of apparent links with Mycenae have been found along with this Apennine material. But the development of Bronze Age cultures seems to have been extremely limited in Etruria and Latium, the part of Italy which was to take the foremost place in Italian history, and which primarily interests us.

The art of working in iron made a sudden début at the beginning of the first millennium and new settlements developed almost everywhere. Cremation became predominant in the north and west of the country. The Iron Age culture in eastern

[1] See Bibliography, p. 153 (Puglisi, S. M.).

Emilia is often called 'Villanovan', after Villanova, the town near Bologna round which characteristic cemeteries were dis, covered about a century ago, and which have since been scientifically investigated. Since the vitally important excava, tions initiated by Count Cozzadini, this new type of culture has increasingly come to be considered by scholars as of the greatest significance. It is found, with the same characteristics, in both the Po valley, where it first appeared, and Etruria and Latium. The recent discoveries at Fermo have revealed it in the Marches, too; and it appears to extend as far as Sicily, at Milazzo. Its extent and importance have attracted great atten, tion and the *Deputazione per la Storia Patria* which has its headquarters at Bologna has devoted to it a book,[1] which also serves as a commemoration of the first find, made a century ago.

Fig. 1

Villanovan culture can be subdivided into various successive stages which, though discernible elsewhere, are most clearly differentiated in the region around Bologna. The Bronze Age was immediately followed by the 'San Vitale' phase; then came the phases of 'Benacci I' and 'Benacci II' which covered, roughly, the whole of the eighth century B.C.; finally the 'Arnoaldi' phase which lasted until the middle of the sixth century and did not disappear until the Etruscans invaded the Po valley. It is not possible here to give a detailed account of this interesting cultural evolution. Typical Villanovan (Benacci I) is characterized by biconical cinerary urns of *impasto* pottery containing the ashes of the dead. The incised decoration is inspired by geometrical patterns. There are also large quantities of ornamental objects and bronze and iron weapons. During the Benacci II (or advanced Villanovan) period bronze urns replaced the pottery ones, and the number of objects, parti, cularly those imitating eastern models, increased. The Arnoaldi period was deeply influenced by Etruria, then at the height of its prosperity. The cultures of the Venetian region and

[1] *Civiltà del Ferro.* See Bibliography, p. 153.

Fig. 1   Iron Age civilization in the Italian peninsula

Lombardy, closely related to the Villanovan, have been given the respective names of Atestine and Golaseccan.

A brilliant culture of the Villanovan type also developed in Etruria and Latium, which had seen so little activity in the previous period—a culture which is of the greatest significance with regard to Etruscan origins as well as the birth of Rome. Cremation became the predominant form of burial throughout the country; pit-graves were dug into the ground and each contained its biconical urn. Some of the cemeteries have a particularly archaic appearance which links them with the late Apennine period. The primitive tombs of Allumiere near Civita Vecchia, for instance, must be compared to those of San Vitale at Bologna. On Etruscan territory cemeteries and dwelling-places grew up on the sites which were soon to be occupied by the great Tuscan cities. The burial offerings, pottery vases, fibulae, necklaces, bronze ornaments and iron weapons indicate that technical knowledge was already considerable and that the urban groups enjoyed a steady prosperity. During an advanced stage of the Villanovan period, from the eighth century B.C. onwards, *fossa*-graves appeared, necessitated by burial customs, the number and quality of ornamental objects increased and the use of silver and gold became more common. Side by side with *impasto* pottery there were vases of light terracotta with painted geometrical decoration in imitation of Greek models.

The same process, to which we shall return later, occurred in Latium and on the site of Rome itself. But in these regions the Villanovan type of culture had a particular character known

Plates 23–41

as Latial, which is evidenced in Rome itself in the *sepolcreto* of the Forum, the cemeteries on the Alban hills, at Anzio and elsewhere. This distinctive character is shown in certain vase

Fig. 8

forms, as for instance the *olle* decorated with raised ridges forming a sort of network, in the comparative poverty of the decoration engraved on the vases, in a certain archaic quality in the weapons and fibulae, and in the large number of hut urns

which take the place of biconical cinerary urns. The hut urn, which is also common in southern Etruria, is to be found all over the Alban hills and at Rome, and bears witness to a clearly defined funerary symbolism. The remains of the deceased were placed in an object made in the form of the house occupied by the individual when alive; this parallelism between the house of the living and the house of the dead, and, in more general terms, between existence in this world and in the next, is found in a highly developed state throughout the history of Etruria and the *Urbs* itself. The hut urn also furnishes valuable evidence, as we shall see, about the exact structure of the primitive dwellings of the 'first Romans'. *Figs. 5, 10, 11*
Plate 33

In the eastern part of central Italy and the south, the Iron Age culture, far from being rigidly separated from the preceding period, seems to have been an imperceptible transformation of Apennine culture. Its characteristics vary according to the region concerned, differing as between northern Picenum (with the discovery of Novilara) and southern Picenum, Umbria, the Abruzzi, Apulia and the south of the peninsula from Campania to Calabria. The links between eastern Italy and the countries on the other side of the Adriatic are striking. The exhibits in the newly renovated National Museum of the Marches give a clear picture of the great wealth of the Picenian Iron Age cultures. Stone weapons had completely disappeared, bronze and iron were widely used, and large fibulae, in broken arc or disk form, became more and more numerous. Most important of all, tombs were mainly in *fossa*-form and the practice of inhumation continued to hold sway almost exclusively.

THE DISTRIBUTION OF PEOPLES IN ANCIENT ITALY

The obscurity surrounding the history of the ancient peoples of Italy until the eighth century B.C., which was only partially dissipated by archaeological evidence, is beginning to clear a little. The Greeks who, from the middle of the eighth century B.C., began to settle on the shores of Magna Graecia and Sicily brought with them a culture which had existed at an advanced level in the eastern Mediterranean for centuries; their written traditions are of invaluable assistance to us in illuminating the history of the peoples of Italy. Thanks to their influence and that of the Etruscans, who began to infiltrate into the centre of the peninsula in 700 B.C., the seeds of progress were sown throughout the country. The Iron Age cultures developed both on the material and on the spiritual and mental plane. The large urban centres increased in number and their buildings improved. The written language developed in the different regions, so that it is possible for a linguistic plan of the country and a territorial plan of the different peoples to be drawn up. The most rapid transformations took place in the south owing to the immediate presence of Hellenism; consequently it is most convenient to follow the map of Italy from south to north, starting with the regions which first received the benefits of colonization.

Fig. 2

Literary, epigraphic and archaeological sources all point to the presence on the coasts of Sicily and Sardinia of merchants of Phoenician origin, from at least the eighth century B.C. Phoenician trade needed ports of call and storage depots along its Spanish and African trading routes. The rapid development of the Phoenician city, Carthage, on the coast of Africa, transformed these bases into permanent establishments, out of which grew Lilybaeum, Motya, Eryx, Palermo, Soluntum and Cefalu in Sicily, and Cagliari, Nora and Sulci in the south-west of Sardinia. None of these colonies, which were later to serve as apples of discord between Phoenicia and Greece, and then between Rome and Carthage, developed a really original art or culture; they were principally transmitting agents for Greek culture, by which they were strongly influenced. However, Phoenician commerce brought with it numerous

Fig. 2   The peoples of Italy in the historic period

oriental luxury objects which found favour first with the Etruscans, then with the Latins, in the seventh and sixth centuries B.C.

In the ethnic, political and cultural spheres the Greek colonists settled on Italian soil exercised an influence of quite a different kind. Its extent and depth is frequently emphasized by Greek historians such as Herodotus, Thucydides, Diodorus Siculus and Strabo, and it can be deduced from innumerable objects of all kinds found on the sites of towns and cemeteries. As early as the eighth century the Chalcidians of Euboea, Greeks of Ionian stock, had founded Naxos, Zancle, Leontini and Catania in Sicily, Rhegium in the toe of the peninsula and Cumae in Campania. The Dorians ran them close. Corinth founded Syracuse, Megara created Megara Hyblaea. On the Ionian coast of Italy the Dorians of Achaea founded the colonies of Croton, Sybaris and Metapontum, while those of Sparta founded Tarentum. By collating archaeological dis-coveries with traditional beliefs one can arrive at a fairly accurate idea of the dates and course of development of their foundations. The older colonies belonging to Magna Graecia founded, in their turn, new and important cities such as Selinus and Agrigentum in Sicily, and Paestum in Cam-pania. The cities of southern Italy remained disunited but in Sicily the fierce struggles against Carthage promoted Syracusan supremacy which was undisputed at the beginning of the fifth century under the tyranny of Dionysius. The cultural contri-bution of the western Greeks settled on Italian soil cannot be over-emphasized. It was due to them that scholarship, philosophy, poetry, military and civil architecture and the arts in general blossomed out brilliantly in the south of Italy, often with an original character quite unlike that of the mother country. In this way the techniques, religion and art of the Italian peoples were decidedly and permanently influenced.

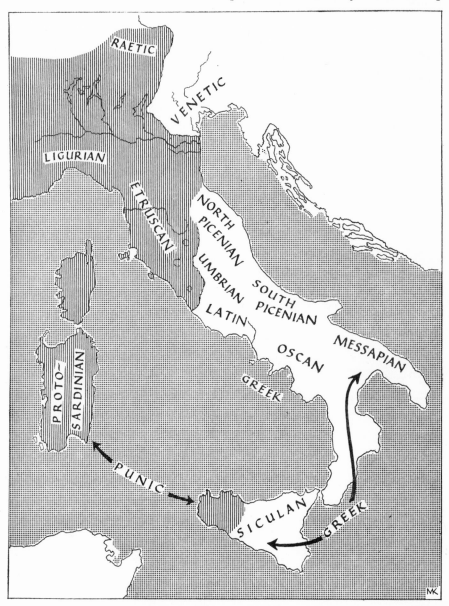

Fig. 3 Languages and dialects of Italy in about 700. The shaded area indicates the non-Indo-European linguistic field

Fig. 3

Both the Phoenicians and Carthaginians on the one hand and the Greeks on the other found themselves thrown, by force of circumstances, into contact with native peoples of whose origin we know little. Classical texts speak of ethnic links between the Sardinians and the tribes of Africa and Spain. Only a few traces of the Sardinian language remain, and these are mainly either toponymic or lexical, but they are definitely of ancient Mediterranean origin. From the second millennium B.C. the Sardinians possessed a native culture; its most imposing remains are the *nuraghi*, cyclopean monuments of circular form. At the start of the Phoenician colonization this culture was at its height and it has left numerous examples of a plastic art

consisting of bronzes in a striking original style. The tribes in the interior of the island, the Ilienses, put up a savage resistance to invasions, both those of the Carthaginians and the later attempts of the Romans. According to the Greek historians, the whole of Sicily was occupied in the beginning by the Sicani; later the Siculi arrived on the scene and pushed back the earlier occupants towards the west. Both the Sicani and the Elymi appear to have been of pre-Indo-European origin and from the Mediterranean area, to judge from the place-name evidence available. The Siculi infiltrated into southern Italy as well as into Sicily. Their language was of Indo-European character, as is shown by surviving inscriptions and ancient glosses on Siculan words. They settled in the island at a very early date; their Iron Age culture is best shown by the rock-cut cemeteries at Pinocchito, near Noto.

Little is known about the ancient peoples of Lucania, Campania and the region now known as Calabria. Reading from south to north, they were the Itali, whose name was to be unexpectedly perpetuated, the Oenotrians, the Bruttians, the Osci and the Ausones. A few onomastic remains, coin inscriptions, seem to indicate a relationship between their dialects on the one hand and Siculan inscriptions and Latin on the other.

This fact has given rise to the hypothesis that there existed along the Tyrrhenian coast, from the Tiber to Sicily, a spread of peoples interrelated amongst themselves and distinct from the Italic strains of the east. Accordingly, there must have been another series of peoples (now grouped under the name of Protolatins), besides the Umbro-Sabellians, from the Apennine and Adriatic regions and probably of an earlier date. The individual character of the more southerly of these tribes was completely counteracted by Greek, Etruscan and East Italic expansion.

Apulia, called in ancient times Iapygia, was the home of the Iapyges. Near them were the Messapians, Peucetians and Daunians, all of whom were held by the Ancients to be of foreign origin. The large number of inscriptions in the Greek alphabet found on Apulian territory shows that the Iapygian tongue was Indo-European, but unrelated to the Italic idioms and closely akin to Illyrian. This seems to confirm the traditional view that the Iapyges were of Balkan origin. Their culture was, of course, much influenced by the Greek colonies in the area and in particular, Tarentum. It is mainly known from burial-places ranging from the eighth to the third century B.C., and its most characteristic form is a style of painted pottery with geometric decoration. The vases often have very tall handles. The most important cities, Canosa, Ruvo and Brindisi were united by federal links, enabling them to put up a stubborn resistance against the Greeks; they succumbed only to the Roman legions.

The centre of Italy was occupied by many peoples, some of which were to exercise a decisive influence on the history of the peninsula. This book will be mainly concerned with the culture of the ancient Latins, living at the mouth of the Tiber, but it is necessary to give at least a rough idea of the importance to Italian primitive history of the Etruscans, who called themselves *Rasenna* or *Rasna* and were called *Tyrrhenoi* by the

Greeks. It was the name given them by the Latins, *Tusci* or *Etrusci*, which eventually descended to Tuscany, the province which they were the first to develop. The Etruscan culture came into being about 700 B.C. It followed the Villanovan culture which had had a brief floruit in Tuscany. Chamber, tombs, topped by false vaults or domes, and often dug under huge barrows or tumuli, became common. Apart from a few regions such as Clusium, cremation gave way to inhumation. There are signs of an unusual and almost unparalleled wealth in towns like Cerveteri or Palestrina; the jewellery is of an oriental refinement and luxury. This stage of their culture, commonly known as the orientalizing period, marks the beginning of Etruscan history.

The problem of Etruscan origins continues to divide scholars. Did they come by sea from Asia Minor, as Herodotus believed (1, 94), or were they an aboriginal race, as postulated by Dionysius of Halicarnassus (1, XXV to XXX)? The post-classical theory that the Etruscans came from the north and entered Italy via the Alps has now been almost abandoned. The tendency today is to look for the origin of the new civiliza, tion in cultural influences, commercial links and the conjunc, tion of favourable circumstances, and to attribute only a secondary importance to a hypothetical migration which, according to available documentation, cannot be rejected. Our knowledge of the Etruscan language, spoken in Tuscany until near the beginning of the Christian era, derives from a linen book (the text on the wrappings of the Zagreb mummy) and some ten thousand inscriptions, most of them short and repeti, tive. By dint of perseverance scholars have managed to make out the phonetics and morphology of the language but the longer texts remain obscure. As far as is known, there is no language directly related to Etruscan and, in the absence of bilingual texts, many Etruscan writings are still untrans, latable. Although influenced by Indo-European tongues, it is

Plate 53

certain that Etruscan does not belong to the Indo-European family.

The progress of Etruscan culture was rapid, almost start-lingly so, and prior to about 500 B.C. there were two centuries of great prosperity and power. The exploitation of Tuscan mines led to continual communication with Greece and the east; a navy came into being to protect security and trade. Their alliance with Carthage enabled the Etruscans to hold their own against Greek ships. Moreover, there was expansion on land as well as at sea. During the second half of the sixth century the Po valley was subjugated and colonized. At the same time Latium and Campania fell under Tuscan rule. But both on land and sea there was a swift and early decline of power. The defeat at Cumae in 474 marked the end of their ephemeral maritime supremacy. They lost Latium at the beginning of the fifth century and shortly afterwards Campania fell to the Osco-Sabellians. In the fourth century the Celts gained possession of the Po valley. And soon afterwards Etruria herself yielded to the pressure of the Roman legions.

From the beginning the essentially urban Etruscan culture stood out from the agricultural and pastoral way of life of the Italic peoples. As an Italian phenomenon it was highly original, a fact which struck even the Ancients. Its originality is most evident in the sphere of religion and in its general conception of the world and the destiny of man. But historically speaking, Etruria was essentially an intermediary; its people assimilated Hellenic creations with disconcerting facility and transmitted them to neighbouring peoples. It did little to 'Etruscanize' the Italic and Latin peoples, but from an early date it introduced them to a certain amount of Greek influence. No doubt its own traditions were too remote from Italico-Roman ideas to modify them greatly. On the other hand, Hellenism, whose merits it recognized and absorbed, was easy for the peoples of the peninsula to understand and gradually assimilate. But it

Plates 43, 52

35

Fig. 21

does not do to be too dogmatic, for Rome at least retained certain aspects of Etrurian customs, religion and art from the time when she was under Etrurian domination.

In the centre of the peninsula was a series of peoples making up an ethnic and linguistic unity; they are commonly known as the eastern Italics or Umbro-Sabellians. In the south, the Abruzzi were occupied by the Samnites who later spread into Lucania, Calabria and Campania, where they took the name

Plate 4

of Osci. In the centre were the Vestini, the Peligni, the Aequi, the Marsi, the Volsci and the Sabines. In the north, the Umbrians lived in the region to which they have bequeathed their name. The Ancients traced the diffusion of the Osco-Umbrian peoples to the rite of the 'sacred spring', when a whole generation was sacrificed by being forced to emigrate and find a new country. However, historiography offers only confused evidence as to the family relationships linking the various tribes. More is to be gained from a study of linguistics, which reveals the essential unity of the eastern Italic languages and the distance separating them from Latin. Those of the south were all variations of Sabellic or Oscan, known to us from many inscriptions in Samnium, Campania and southern Italy. The most important of these texts are engraved on the *cippus* of Abella and the bronze table of Bantia. In the north the linguistic group is represented by Umbrian, the language used in Umbrian inscriptions, in particular those on the famous bronze tables of Gubbio. The bronze table of Velletri is inscribed in the Volscian dialect.

Despite their ethnic and linguistic ties, the histories of these peoples differ widely. The Samnites, a warlike mountain-race, invaded Campania at the end of the fifth century, then Calabria, and finally Sicily. They did not acknowledge Roman dominion until the end of the long series of wars to which they gave their name. Their culture progressed slowly and, unlike that of the Campanians and Lucanians, was not greatly influenced by the Greeks and Etruscans. The Samnites were closely linked with other central Italian tribes, the Marrucini, Vestini, Peligni and Marsi; not so the Sabines, Aequi and Volsci, who came into early and intimate contact with Etrusco-Latin culture. The Umbrians certainly took their name from the non-Italic tribes which had occupied their territory before them. At a very early stage they came under Etruscan influence. The long text on the Iguvine tables gives much information about their religious customs and political institutions. Some of their towns, such as Gubbio, Todi and Spoleto, enjoyed considerable prosperity.

The Italic peoples of the eastern part of the country pene-trated as far as the territory along the Adriatic coast which corresponds to the Marches of today. But traces have also been found of non-Italic tribes to whom archaeologists have agreed to give the name of Picenians. South of Ancona, a rich Iron Age culture, showing distinct affinities with the cultures of the Balkans, flourished during the seventh and sixth centuries. The tombs at Piceno and Cupramarittima contain beautiful examples of pottery and bronze- and iron-work. In the same region the inscriptions are in a language which though un-doubtedly Indo-European shows definite links with Illyrian languages. Farther north the cemeteries of Novilara, near Pesaro, reveal materials and customs related to those used in the Balkan cultures; the inscriptions on the primitively decorated stelae are in an obscure and unclassifiable dialect. It would seem, therefore, that a large number of the so-called Picenian tribes came from the opposite shore of the Adriatic. The Iapuzco people mentioned on the Iguvine tables naturally leads one to think of the Iapodes of Illyria and the Iapygians of southern Italy.

Fig. 3

Beyond Etruscan territory, in northern Tuscany, Liguria, Piedmont and a part of Lombardy, there was a different group of peoples, known to the Ancients as the Ligures. For certain

Greeks of the archaic period this term actually meant all the peoples of western Europe. Various Ligurian tribes emigrated to the Apennines, Alps and Po valley: the Friniates, the Veiturii (round Genoa), the Ingauni, the Segovii, the Taurini, the Salassi, the Lepontii and others. It is difficult to decide whether these peoples were of common origin. Place-name evidence and classical glosses on Ligurian words indicate that in general the Ligurians were descended from a Mediterranean and pre-Indo-European substratum from western Europe. The Celtic invasions, to which we shall refer later, gave rise to mixed ethnic groups known as Celto-Ligurian, who were probably responsible for the late Lepontic inscriptions that have been found in Upper Lombardy and Ticino. Etruscan expansion and the arrival of the Celts drove back the Ligurians into hiding-places in the Alps or Apennines from which they put up a stubborn resistance to the Romans. The archaeological remains attributed to these ancient tribes do not present a unified picture. Among them are the curious rock drawings of Monte Bego in the Alpes Maritimes, the 'statue menhirs' of Corsica and the drawings engraved on the rocks in the Val Camonica.

Farther east, Etruscan colonization has obscured our know-ledge, as it did that of classical times, concerning the occupants of the alpine and sub-alpine regions above the Po valley. It seems likely that the sub-alpine region was first occupied by the Euganei, the valleys of the Trentino and Upper Adige by the Raeti. Place-name evidence, in fact, indicates the presence of a linguistic layer peculiar to these regions: it is generally called Raetic or Raeto-Euganean and is of a pre-Indo-European type.

The Veneti, who gave their name to their region, occupied the north-east of Italy. In classical times they were thought to be of Illyrian origin. Our knowledge of their language, in which many funerary and votive inscriptions were written, has been greatly increased recently by studies carried out in France and Italy. Most of these inscriptions were discovered in and around

Este, Padua and the Carnic Alps. The language is an Indo-European dialect of archaic character which offers interesting analogies with Latin. The Venetic culture retained certain characteristics of the eighth century B.C. until the time of its Romanization. It reached its peak about 400 B.C., the hey-day of the great centres of Padua and Este; this period is characterized by interesting bronze situlae with repoussé decoration. The wide barriers of the Lower Po and Adige saved Venetic independence from falling a prey to Etruscan or Celtic ambition, so that in the third century B.C. the maritime merchant state was in a position to enter an alliance with Rome on its own terms.

The last important modification of the ethnic scheme in primitive Italy occurred when the Celts invaded the Po valley; they continued till the end of the third century B.C. to make threatening sorties into the rest of the peninsula. Classical authors painted a vivid picture of the terror which seized the country on the arrival of the Celtic warriors, tall, powerful and still half savage. The Gaulish attacks provided some of the most dramatic moments of Roman history. There is, however, considerable doubt as to the date of the Celts' arrival in Italy, their place of origin and the routes they followed. Livy's account (Livy, V, 34) follows the traditional view: about 600 B.C. Ambigatus, king of a Celtic people from Gaul, forced a number of his subjects to leave the country to relieve over-population. An expedition led by his nephew Bellovesus and made up of Bituriges, Arverni, Senones and other Gaulish tribes conquered the Po valley. Later invasions brought the Cenomani to the Brescia-Verona region, the Boii and Lingones to the area west of Milan, the Senones to Tuscany and even Latium itself. All this was supposed to have happened between 600 and the fourth century B.C., but according to archaeology such early dates are not warranted.[1] Judging from the material

[1] *The Celts* by T. G. E. Powell, London, 1958, deals with this in some detail.

found in the numerous Celtic tombs in the north of the peninsula, the main body of the Celts did not enter Italy until the fifth century B.C., though there may have been a few small earlier incursions. The successive waves of invasions must, therefore, have taken place roughly between 450 and 350 B.C.

According to Livy the Celts who invaded Italy came from Gaul. In fact they must have come from Central Europe (Bohemia). At the same period other Celtic tribes were moving in other directions. The cause of these various migrations was the pressure exerted on the Central European Celts by the Germani arriving from the north and east. After crossing the Alpine passes, the invaders fell upon the Etruscans and wrested the Po valley from them. Nevertheless, the population was not completely wiped out and pockets of Etruscan culture sur-vived in parts of upper Italy, such as Mantua. Similarly, there were genuine ethnic fusions on Ligurian territory. The Celts were divided up regionally: the Insubres occupied central Lombardy, the Cenomani the Bergamo-Brescia region, the Boii—who gave to the town called Felsina by the Etruscans the new name of Bononia, which became Bologna—southern Lombardy and Emilia, the Lingones Romagna, and the Senones the north of Picenum which acquired the name of *ager gallicus*. It was not until the second century B.C. that Rome managed to subdue all these peoples.

During their sojourn in the Po valley, the Celts introduced various forms characteristic of the central European Iron Age culture, known as the La Tène culture, after the name of a Swiss site. Their weapons—swords and lances—were well and strongly made, but nevertheless their art and culture (which borrowed freely from the Etruscans) was a distinct retrogression from the level already reached by the peoples occupying the Po valley. Various objects, including luxurious gold articles, have been found in the Celtic tombs, which were first inhumation, later cremation, graves. In general, the Celtic archaeology

of the Po valley offers a fascinating subject of study to anyone with time to analyse the magnificent collections of the
museums of the Marches. Continental Celtic, the language of
the invaders, left only a few traces, like the inscriptions at
Novara and Todi and some onomastic and toponymic evidence.
But it gave certain technical terms to Latin, such as those
concerning various types of chariots and vehicles, which the
Celts were past-masters at making. It is from Celtic, through
Latin and French, that we get the word 'chariot' and its
derivatives.

The above general picture, though necessarily much
abridged, suffices to give an idea of the great cultural and
linguistic complexity of affairs in Italy at the dawn of historical
times. It is impossible fully to understand the origins of the
people of Latium and Rome without setting them within the
framework of the wider Italian scene. Rome at its beginnings
was part and parcel of Italian protohistory, and this alone can
explain the first tentative experiments of a small town beset on
all sides by powerful neighbours from which it received the
first germs of its culture.

CHAPTER III

The Legend of the Origins of Rome: its Formation and Value

THE ORIGINS OF ALL ANCIENT PEOPLES, places and religions are surrounded by legends and myths. But none of these legends has become as well-known and important as that concerning the birth of Rome. It is not easy to separate truth from fiction. Nowadays, however, by correlating the various sources of knowledge at their disposal, scholars have managed to throw light on the formation of these myths, their evolution and the political and religious uses to which they were put at various stages of Rome's history.

But here again one must remember that, despite the centuries of scholarly attention devoted to them, the origins of Rome were not an isolated entity but an integral part of the whole great, complex pattern made up by the early beginnings of the Italic peoples. This broad picture, with its many invasions, derives from Book I of Dionysius of Halicarnassus's *Roman Antiquities*, and from various fragments, unfortunately very incomplete, by Greek and Roman authors, such as Herodotus, Thucydides, Antiochus of Syracuse, Timaeus, Cato, Polybius, Diodorus Siculus, Strabo, Virgil, Pliny the Elder and Servius, to name only the most valuable sources. A kind of legendary history of pre-Roman Italy existed within the larger movement of Greek historiography in the fifth century B.C. Whereas we now know that this network of highly coloured narratives is not to be taken as purely factual history nor as purely mythical ethnology, modern scholars disagree when it comes to separating the mythical background from the real events embedded in it. An interesting idea has recently been suggested: namely, that many apparently invented particulars concerning the arrival of peoples and their chiefs in Italy can be explained as a reflection of the factual Indo-Europeanization of the tribes of the peninsula.

The aim of this chapter is to trace the Roman legend step by step, as it is to be found portrayed in the admirable works of Livy and Virgil and to see how it can be accounted for. For this purpose the best starting-point is the passage in which Livy betrayed both his prudent scepticism and his pride in being a Roman:

> As for the events which immediately preceded the founding of Rome or even the idea of her foundation, the traditions embellished with poetic legends rather than founded on authentic documents, I do not intend either to endorse or to reject them. It is permissible for the ancients to mingle the supernatural with human reality to make the origin of towns more impressive; and besides, if ever a nation had the right to sanctify its origin and attribute it to divine intervention, surely Rome's greatness is enough to make the human race accept the claim without difficulty, as it accepts the city's present authority, when she traces her birth and that of her founder to the god Mars.

In fact, of course, there are two legends, distinguishing between two different periods: the first colonization of Latium, when Lavinium was founded by the Trojan Aeneas, and the foundation of Rome herself by Romulus.

The Trojan legend, immortalized by Virgil, is familiar to everyone. After escaping from the fall of Troy, traditionally dated 1184 B.C., Aeneas undertook a long voyage during which he was constantly pursued by the hatred of Juno, the goddess hostile to the Trojans. At last he and his companions reached the mouth of the Tiber. Sacred omens told him that he had at last found the land marked out for him by fate, the land where it was his mission to found a new city. Aeneas was of divine descent, for although his father, Anchises, was a

Plates 3, 8, 9

mortal, his mother, Venus, was a goddess. Anchises had died during the long voyage, but Aeneas was accompanied by his son, Iulus, or Ascanius, and he had brought with him the Penates, the patron divinities of Troy, which were now to guarantee the destiny of a new city.

The king of the country, Latinus, ruled over a people called the Aborigines; Aeneas won the hand of his daughter Lavinia. He then allied himself with Evander, the Corinthian who had founded the ancient city of Pallanteum, which was to grow into Rome, on the Palatine Hill. Strengthened by this alliance, Aeneas was able to withstand the attacks of a Latin tribe, the Rutuli, whose king, Turnus, was a fellow-suitor for the hand of Lavinia. The Etruscan people of Caere had supported the Trojan army, while the ex-king of Caere, Mezentius, who had been expelled by his subjects, had taken Turnus's side. Turnus and Mezentius were both killed in the fighting. Then Aeneas founded a town which he called Lavinium after Lavinia, not far from the mouth of the Tiber. After his death, Iulus-Ascanius, Aeneas's son by his first wife, Creusa (according to certain traditions he had two sons, one by Creusa, the other by Lavinia), abandoned the governorship of Lavinium and founded Alba Longa at the foot of the Alban hills. He was succeeded by twelve kings whose combined reigns filled the three centuries between the founding of Alba and that of Rome. The last king of this dynasty was Amulius, who dethroned his elder brother, Numitor, and forced his niece (i.e. Numitor's daughter), Rhea Silvia, to become a Vestal Virgin, in order to prevent her from having a son who could one day avenge his grandfather. But, miraculously, the god Mars himself was united with Rhea Silvia, and of the union were born the twins Romulus and Remus, to the first of whom went the honour of founding Rome.

Plate 10

There is no archaeological evidence to support the theory of immigrants arriving on the plains of Latium, nor of the presence in the region of a fairly advanced culture at the date when, according to legend, Aeneas arrived in Italy. The mythical account, then, seems not to be based on a memory of actual facts, though we cannot be sure. The theme can be found in various other legendary accounts connected with the earliest periods in Italy. In several of them a hero comes from beyond the seas, marries the daughter of the local sovereign and so inherits his father-in-law's power. Thus in Lycophron and his commentators and in Antoninus Liberalis, Diomedes arrives on the coast of Apulia with his companions; he is welcomed by the king, Daunus, helps him to conquer his enemies, the Messapians, and is rewarded with the hand of the king's daughter and half the kingdom. Similarly, in Diodorus Siculus (V, 8), Aeolus, banished from Metapontum, sails across the Tyrrhenian Sea, lands on the island of Lipari, marries King Liparo's daughter and succeeds to the throne. In both cases the new arrivals mingle on equal terms with the native population. It is clear, therefore, that the form of the narrative is a common one, but that its various versions arose out of differing circum-stances. Although it is unlikely that the Mycenaeans formed true colonies in Italy at so early a date, the coming and going of merchants and the existence of a regular trade with Mycenaean Greece may account for certain of these stories. But at the present moment archaeological evidence does not warrant this explan-ation of the Aeneas legend; the answer must be sought elsewhere.

One theory, based solely on textual criticism, attributes a recent date to the birth of the legend and suggests that it was formulated as a result of Pyrrhus of Epirus's Italian expedition at the beginning of the third century B.C. But systematic com-parison of the textual, linguistic, topographical and archae-ological evidence has led to other, and apparently definitive, conclusions. The archaeological material found in Etruria, which includes illustrations of Aeneas fleeing from his country, shows that the Aeneas-figure was known to the Tuscan people

Plate 3

as early as the sixth century B.C. This had already been suggested by the terracotta statuettes of Aeneas bearing his father,
Anchises, on his shoulders, found at Veii, about nine miles
from Rome. The dating of the statuettes is not certain and is
still open to discussion, but comparisons with a whole series
of other objects put the whole matter beyond doubt. A sixth-
century Etruscan scarab in the Cabinet des Médailles in Paris
shows Aeneas bearing his father on his shoulders. Moreover,
out of eleven Greek vases showing the same scene and dating
from the last quarter of the sixth century, five come from
Etruria, one from Campania, one from Spina, an Etruscan
town at the mouth of the Po; the origin of the others is un-
certain. In itself, the presence of these particular Greek vases on
Etruscan territory is significant. It would seem that they were
imported to satisfy a public to whom the theme shown was
both familiar and popular. Therefore, the Trojan warrior must
have been known in central Italy before 500 B.C.

These objects show only the scene of the hero fleeing his
country with his father. It is possible that the legend concerning
his arrival in Italy, and more particularly in Latium, was
stimulated by an ancient place-name, Troia, the name of the
coast of Latium between Ardea and Lavinium (Cato, fragment 8). There was a similar place-name in Venetia. It has also
been suggested that a verbal similarity could lie behind the story
of the portent seen by Aeneas on his arrival in Latium, the appari-
tion of the wild sow with thirty piglets. But this apparently attractive explanation of the sow (*troia* in Latin) appearing in the Troia
region is rendered unlikely by the age of the word *troia* (=sow),
which is not to be found in the texts of the time and, in fact,
appears for the first time in the eighth-century *Gloses de Cassel*.

However, both in the ancient texts and the pictorial illustrations of the sixth century, Aeneas appears as a pious man who
in his flight takes with him his father and the gods of his
country, the Penates. At its very beginnings, therefore, the

46

legend had the same character which it retained throughout its future history. But why and how did it grow up in Etruria? In the absence of definite evidence the question is difficult to answer. One after another the Elymi (a little-known Sicilian people), the Campanians and the Etruscans themselves have been suggested as prime movers in the creation of the myth. One attractive hypothesis suggests the Phocaeans who, hard pressed by the Persians, came from Asia Minor to the Tyr-rhenian coast in large numbers in the sixth century; they came into close contact with the Etruscans and became their avowed enemies. It is possible that Rome itself, then an Etrusco-Latin town, got the legend of the Trojan Aeneas from them and then adapted it to its own needs, making Aeneas into the founder of Rome. Already, at this early period, Rome's choice showed her predilection for the particular virtue which throughout her long history was to be considered of most importance for private citizen and public man alike: *pietas*, pious attachment to one's parents and the gods. *Pietas* was to be one of the major   Plates 3, 8, 9
themes of Augustan propaganda. It can be seen magnificently illustrated in the bas-reliefs decorating the wall surrounding two of the finest imperial altars, the *Ara Pacis*, built by Augustus himself, and the *Ara Pietatis*, erected by Claudius to the memory of Livia and the founder of the Empire.

The second part of the legend about the founding of Rome poses completely different problems. To take up the traditional story where we left it: when Amulius, the great-uncle of Romulus and Remus, learned of their birth, he decided to kill them in order to stamp out the danger they represented. So he ordered them to be thrown into the Tiber, according to ancient custom, near the fig-tree called Ruminal. But the current gently washed the twins on to the bank, where they were found and fed, in a miraculous way, by a she-wolf in the cave of the   Plates 5, 7
Lupercal, at the south-west corner of the Palatine Hill. Soon

afterwards they were found by a shepherd and shepherdess, Faustulus and Larentia, who brought them up in their modest, rustic home. When they had reached adolescence, Romulus and Remus killed the usurper Amulius and gave back the throne of Alba to its legal owner, their grandfather, Numitor. Later they left their town to found a new city.

They came to the site on which Rome was later to be built. It was, in fact, the place where they had been cast into the river and where they had spent their childhood. To find out who the gods intended should found the city they took the auspices, Romulus on the Palatine Hill, Remus on the Aventine.

Remus was the first to receive an omen [says Livy]; he saw six vultures. He had just pointed it out, when Romulus saw double the number. Each was proclaimed king by his own side. Remus based his claim to the throne on priority, Romulus on the larger number of birds. They argued, came to blows; tempers were roused and degenerated into blood-lust. Remus was killed during the fighting. On the other hand, according to a more popular tradition, Remus, to make fun of his brother, jumped the newly built walls at one bound and Romulus angered, killed him, adding: 'So shall perish all who attempt to pass over our walls.' Thus the power fell into Romulus's hands alone, and after its foundation the town took the name of its founder.

Other authors, such as Ovid in Book IV of the *Fasti*, describe in detail the rites practised during the actual founda-tion. Romulus marked out the line of the city walls by plough-ing a furrow round the Palatine with a ploughshare. Harnessed to it were a pure white cow and bull. Along this primordial furrow the citizens then laid the foundations of the new wall. This was the origin of the *pomoerium* of the city, the sacrosanct, taboo zone that surrounded the main body of the city with an

Plate 14

effectual frontier protected by its divine associations. The entire history of Rome dates from this basic ceremony, which took place on April 21, 747, according to some, 753 according to others. Each year April 21 was commemorated by a solemn and ancient ceremonial on the Palatine, the ritual of the *Palilia* (or *Parilia*) dedicated to Pales, the pastoral god. The aim of this shepherds' feast was to ensure the safety and fertility of the animals, and it was inevitably linked with the memory of the time when the prosperity of the new village depended on its herds.

In a later chapter we shall analyse the recent discoveries on the Palatine which have revealed a group of hut-foundations dating from about the middle of the eighth century, a period that would correspond with Romulus's early settlement, as described in the legend. It seems, therefore, that the legend masks a historically attested fact and that the myth grew up around accurate memories. These memories were stirred again and again in the daily life of ancient Rome, by a series of religious survivals and place-names. The fig-tree, Ruminal, where the she-wolf suckled the divine twins, and the Lupercal, the sacred cave which sheltered them, were widely worshipped. The place where Romulus took the auspices was known; it was the *auguraculum*. The legend of Evander and Aeneas had already become linked to the Palatine Hill by means of a sort of natural projection of these memories into an even more remote mythological past. According to this additional legend, in the time of Hercules the Arcadian hero Evander had already settled on the brow of the Cermalus. A stairway connecting the Cermalus with the valley of the Circus Maximus was called the *Scalae Caci* (stairway of Cacus) after the giant Cacus who had attempted to rob Hercules of the cattle which the latter had collected during his expedition against Geryon. It is true that Virgil transfers the scene of the Cacus legend to the Aventine, but this was probably an

Plates 15-18

49

innovation of his own, aiming to remove all violent associations from the Palatine, the sacred hill.

In any case, the traditional associations connecting Romulus with the Palatine had yet another significance in the classical period: it was in the Lupercal, the cave south-west of the hill, that the ancient body, the Luperci, met on February 15 to sacrifice a goat. It was from there, too, that the strange race run by these wolf-priests started, 'this wild brotherhood', as Cicero wrote, 'pastoral and rural, of priests dressed as wolves, whose yearly meetings began before civilization or laws' (*Pro Caelio,* 26). The Luperci, dressed only in goatskin loincloths and holding straps made of the skin of the goat sacrificed, started their magic race round the Palatine from the Lupercal; on the way they touched the women with their straps, to make them fertile. This ancient magic ritual of purification and fertility continued until the end of the fifth century A.D. on the hill which was, in fact, the cradle of the oldest Latin settlement; to the end it kept its links with one of the sacred places associated with Romulus's childhood.

Near the *Scalae Caci* there still existed, in classical times, the *casa Romuli* (Romulus's hut), piously preserved and maintained from generation to generation. This ancient monument was sometimes called *tugurium Faustuli* and taken to be the dwelling, not of Romulus himself, but of the shepherd who had given him refuge and thus ensured his safety. Finally, an archaic altar in front of the temple of Apollo on the Palatine Hill com-memorated the foundation ceremony. In Roman literature this altar is called the *Roma quadrata,* and according to Ovid (*Fasti,* V, 819) it was built of a single square stone under which Romulus had placed a sample 'of every object in the world'.

The character of Romulus himself, kept alive by so many associations on and around the Palatine Hill, was a major component of Roman national feeling. Various legends of different dates, often difficult to identify, grew on the one hand into the story of the twins united at first and then rivals to the death; and on the other, that of the figure of the divine king, the founder of the *Urbs*. The myth of the twins who were only divided by the birth of Rome is of Latin origin and apparently dates back only to the second half of the fourth century B.C. Livy writes that the Ogulnii brothers, the *aediles curules*, had a bronze statue of the she-wolf suckling the twins placed near the fig-tree, Ruminal, in 296 B.C. This group was to be a constant symbol of the humble, miraculous beginnings of a city blessed by the gods.

Plates 5-7

But in reality the second twin dropped into a minor position, and the dawning glory of the *Urbs* came to be associated with Romulus alone. In the Annals of Ennius he is already the king-founder, the single *conditor*. Roman historians gradually became more and more interested in his reign, the legendary content of which became progressively more elaborate, in his exploits as a warrior and finally in his apotheosis and diviniza tion. In the first century B.C. there was no lack of ambitious men who, anticipating Augustus, would each have liked to be regarded as a new Romulus. The figure of the first king thus became idealized and was endowed with all the best qualities of the founder, the general and the statesman. The legend became, in a sense, a thing of the present and was injected with new life by becoming a theme of political propaganda. A mystical theology centred round Romulus grew up; its elements have recently been analysed. It glorified the *parens* or *pater patriae*, the predestined founder whose return would herald a new golden age, and the conquering hero, assimilated after his death and apotheosis to the god Quirinus.

The figure of Romulus, consequently, was a useful aid to those who sought power during the troubled, revolutionary period—to Sulla, to Caesar, to Octavian; and its depth and content progressively increased. The new masters of Rome attributed numerous merits to it when they imagined themselves to be achieving something new and beneficial, whether in the political, social or economic spheres. On the other hand, those opposed to dictatorship in any form sought to belittle the hero whom the power-seekers quoted as an authority. For them the first king was a brutal tyrant acting with complete contempt for the law. The ancient Romulus myth thus became a part of modern Roman life, a theme of the greatest urgency to both poles of Roman political consciousness. With the advent of the principate its status was decided and Octavian became, for the world, the Romulus *redivivus* of a re-born and, as it were, newly founded Rome. The theme was taken up again and again in the art and literature of his time.

According to the traditional account there were seven kings, Latin and Sabine until 616, and then Etruscan, between the founding of Rome and the advent of the Republic in 509 B.C. The whole of Livy, Book I, is devoted to telling the deeds of the kings, and this is a suitable place in which to give a brief summary of his full narrative. Myths, legends and history are intricately interwoven in his description of the first centuries in Rome; after summarizing it we shall attempt to unravel the various threads.

According to Varro's long chronology which places the founding of Rome in 753 B.C., Romulus reigned from 753 to 717 B.C. His political and military achievements were consider-able. He converted the area between the two peaks of the Capitol into an 'asylum'. 'To it came a heterogeneous crowd of people from neighbouring regions, a confused mixture of free men and slaves, all seeking novelty, and in this way the numbers of Roman citizens grew to correspond with the majestic scale of the city itself.' (Livy I, 8, 6) He also formed a senatorial body with a hundred members, the *Patres*, whose descendants were to receive the honourable title of *patricii*. The commoners formed an assembly of their own, to which he gave a code of law. He himself adopted various symbols of authority and was, for instance, always preceded by twelve lictors. The

lack of women led him to organize the rape of the Sabines to   Plate 15
provide wives for his companions. This exploit gave rise to a
war with the neighbouring Sabine people. A Vestal Virgin,
Tarpeia, let them into the citadel of the Capitol, and there was   Plate 12
a battle between the Romans and the Sabines in the valley
separating the Palatine from the Capitol, as a result of which
the two peoples decided to amalgamate into one, the Quirites.
Romulus now had to share his power, which until then had
been absolute, with the Sabine king, Titus Tatius. The population was divided into thirty *curiae* or, according to Cicero,
three tribes, the *Ramnenses, Titienses* and *Luceres*. Livy applies
these names only to the three centuries of *equites* created, he says,
by Romulus, who was accompanied by three hundred men,
forming a sort of praetorian guard. During a storm Romulus
mysteriously disappeared and went to join the gods. Or,
according to a version of the story hostile to Romulus, he was
torn to pieces by the *Patres*.

After an interregnum of a year, the senate chose as king a
Sabine from Cures, Numa Pompilius, who reigned from 716
to 673 B.C. He was of a religious caste and was eager for his
power to be confirmed by the gods, as that of Romulus had
been. An augur took the auspices by dividing the sky with his
bent stick, the *lituus*, and found them favourable, after which
Numa was declared king.

As the sovereign of a new city founded by force, he set
about establishing it on new foundations—law, order and
morality. But as he saw that in a state of war these reforms
were impossible because military life fostered pugnacity, he
decided that he could only tame this wild people by breaking
them of the habit of warfare. Therefore he built a temple to
Janus at the foot of the Argiletum to symbolize peace and
war: if it was open it indicated that Rome was at war; if
closed, that there was peace in the city. It was closed only

twice after Numa's reign: once under the consulate of Titus Manlius at the end of the first Punic War, and once—may the gods be thanked, our generation witnessed this occasion —after Actium, by the emperor Caesar Augustus, when he had re-established peace on land and sea. (Livy, I, 19)

He claimed to meet the goddess Egeria every night and to be advised by her, and on this basis built up a solid Roman religious and priestly code. He divided the days into *Fasti* (lawful) and *Nefasti* (unlawful), and the year into twelve months. He created the *flamines* (priests) of Jupiter, Mars and Quirinus, introduced the Alban cult of Vesta to Rome, organized the brotherhood of the Twelve Salii, whose task was to sing and dance, striking their sacred shields with their lances, in honour of Mars Gradivus. He also created a supreme pontifex, charged with absolute control of public and private religion.

The death of Numa was followed by an interregnum after which the people's choice, ratified by the Senate, fell on a Latin called Tullus Hostilius, who reigned from 672 to 641. He was a warlike king and provided a direct contrast with the peace-loving Numa. During his reign were established various hard-and-fast rules, according to which the college of the Fetiales concluded all treaties in the name of Rome. The *foedus* was solemnly confirmed by the sacrifice of a pig, slaughtered by the Pater Patratus by means of a single blow with a stone. These rites were applied in the first treaty which the Romans remembered, according to Livy: this was the treaty in which Alba and Rome, then at war, decided to settle their differences in a single combat between the three Curiatii brothers and the three Horatii brothers. The episode is well known. Two of the three Horatii fell, but the third killed in turn each of his three opponents, who were weakened by their wounds. He then returned to the city, bearing the spoils of all three men; near the Capena gate he met his sister, who was engaged to one of the Curiatii and mourned his death, whereupon he killed her. Indicted by the duumvirs for a crime against the State, he appealed to the people, and his father too took his part. Horatius was acquitted, but his father was ordered to instigate purification ceremonies for his son at the State's expense. These expiatory sacrifices remained a tradition in the Horatian *gens*. The father placed a wooden beam across the road and made his son pass under this yoke-like object with his head veiled. The beam still existed in Livy's time and was known as the *sororium tigillum* (the sister's beam). The magical import of this ancient rite is easily comprehensible: the beam placed in this particular position constituted a sort of sacred doorway and by passing through it Horatius left behind him all his impurity.

A year later, Alba was attacked again. On this occasion the ancient city was completely defeated and destroyed and its inhabitants were taken to swell the number of the Romans. It was then that the Mons Caelius was annexed by the city. Tullus had the *Curia Hostilia* built for the Senate at the foot of the Capitol. Then on the pretext that Roman merchants had been stopped, in violation of the law of nations, at the *lucus Feroniae*, near Capena, he declared war on the powerful Sabines and defeated them. But Jupiter Elicius struck him down, angered because certain rites had been neglected during a sacrifice to him.

After an interregnum of two years Ancus Marcius, the grandson on his mother's side of Numa Pompilius, succeeded to the throne and reigned from 639 to 616 B.C. Just as Numa had codified religious practices in time of peace, so he set about instituting a similar code for war. The ritual accompanying the conclusion of a treaty was already defined. Ancus Marcius borrowed from the ancient nation of the Aequicoli the rules by which the *Fetiales* were to present their just demands. Later he instituted ceremonies to accompany the declaration of war: the *fetialis* was to go to the enemy frontier, recite a sacred formula and throw into the enemy territory a javelin made of cornelwood and having either an iron point or one end sharpened and hardened by fire. This gesture was to ensure a fearsome and magical efficacy.

Ancus Marcius was successful in various wars with neigh﹣bouring Latin towns and brought many thousands of con﹣quered Latins to the Aventine. This hill was then incorporated into the city, along with the Palatine Hill, the cradle of Rome, the Capitol, occupied by the Sabines, and the Caelius, occupied by the people of Alba. The Janiculum was connected to Rome by a wooden bridge, the first to be built over the Tiber. Finally, the colony of Ostia was founded at the mouth of the Tiber.

According to tradition, the death of Ancus Marcius in 616 marked the beginning of the line of Etruscan kings. Since this period was nearer in time to the Roman historians recording it, their recollections are more precise. But it can be seen from the foregoing account that even the earlier reigns reveal, on analysis, various aspects founded in fact. There is no doubt that all the archaic rituals attributed by Livy to the eighth or seventh centuries—the dances of the Salii, the races of the Luperci, the festivals of Pales—can be traced to the earliest periods in Rome; the archaeological evidence and comparisons of these rites with similar ones in neighbouring countries leave no room for doubt. In a later chapter on the religion of ancient Rome one example, that of the Salii, will be studied in detail to bring out this fact more clearly. It is true that Livy's account shows many ana﹣chronisms and that Rome in the eighth and seventh centuries was quite incapable of waging wars on this scale against peoples stronger than herself. My impression, however, is that many of the elements of this ancient tradition will be confirmed, if they have not already been, by archaeological discoveries.

But there is another factor which seems today to add weight to these early historical accounts. From the very beginning the Roman mentality revealed itself as unwilling to accept myths. Compared with the exceptional fertility of the Greeks, the Germans' aptitude for developing cosmic drama and the Celts' taste for heroic and legendary stories, the poverty of Roman myth is surprising. As celebrated in Rome, rites were bare, dry ceremonies denuded of all mythical connotations. Nevertheless, the Indo-European myths had not completely disappeared. They evolved differently in different ethnic milieux. If Indian ideology, for instance, tends to be of a cosmic nature, Roman ideology takes a historical form. In other words, myths and rites take on the shape of historical accounts.

Sometimes it is possible to trace the progression of this religious disintegration in the Roman mind, this 'historisation' of myths. In every case comparisons show that basic Indo-European myths were incorporated into the fabric of primitive history and given a national and moral content.

In Indo-European thought, sovereignty has two aspects: magical and frightening on the one hand, peaceful and law-giving on the other. India has two complementary gods, Varuna the magician and Mitra the law-giver. The same opposition can be found in Scandinavia with Odin and Thor, in Greek mythology with Uranos and Zeus, in the Roman cult itself with Jupiter on the one side and Dius Fidius on the other. But a similar duality also appears in Rome in the persons of her first two kings, Romulus, a violent figure surrounded by the tumultuous brotherhood of the Luperci, and Numa, the wise law-giver, worshipping *Fides*, the good faith. The Scandinavian gods, Odin the one-eyed and Thor the one-armed, are perhaps paralleled by two famous Roman warriors, Horatius Cocles and Mucius Scaevola, who lost respectively an eye and an arm in their fight against the Etruscan Porsenna. Similarly the heroic episode of Horatius vanquishing the three Alban conquerors may well be a very Roman form of the ancient myth symbolizing the warrior's initiation which the Irish legend of Cúchulainn presents in a supernatural guise. Comparative analysis has discovered similar transpositions of mythical fragments in other elements of Roman national history, such as the legend of Tarpeia, the life of Servius Tullius and his links with Fortuna. Certain classifications of the gods and the way in which important priesthoods were organized may well represent survivals of ancient social structures of Indo-European type.

The disintegration of Indo-European myth in the Latin consciousness appears to date back to a very early period. It can be explained by deeply rooted psychological tendencies and the absence of a mythical imagination which was to emerge only later under the influence of the Hellenization of the Roman religion. But to the end the Roman mind remained disinclined to formulate divine genealogies or cosmological systems, and this tendency was fostered by religious importations without much connexion with local tradition, Greek influences introduced without any ritual element to back them, and Etruscan elements which superimposed a layer of foreign religion on the Latin heritage. But the deciding factor in the Romans' use of various disintegrated myths within their primitive history was no doubt their basic tendency—visible throughout their existence, in both religion and art—to consider the whole world from a historical standpoint.

According to tradition, the seventh and sixth centuries B.C. were occupied by the reigns of three Etruscan kings. As related in the epic accounts given by Roman historians, their exploits were as follows. Under the reign of Ancus Marcius, Lucumon, a wealthy citizen of Tarquinii, had settled in Rome. His father, Demaratus, was a Greek from Corinth who had left his country on account of political troubles. Lucumon was married to Tanaquil, an Etruscan lady of high degree. Their arrival in Rome was marked by a significant omen. On the Janiculum an eagle swooped down and removed Lucumon's head-dress. It then hovered round the chariot uttering loud squawks and finally replaced the hat on Lucumon's head. Tanaquil is said to have been gladdened by this incident, for she had the gift, common in Etruria, of divining heavenly omens. Embracing her husband, she urged him to foster great and lofty hopes 'according to the bird which came, the heavenly region from which it came and the god whose messenger it was. The omen referred to the highest part of his body; the eagle had removed an ornament from the head of a man: he replaced it there by order of a god.' (Livy, I, 34, 9) The omen of the eagle takes us into the sphere of divination of which the Etruscans were always fond. As a nation they were familiar with various techniques for deducing the prophecy from the signs sent by the gods. Six centuries later a similar omen heralded Octavius's greatness: an eagle, according to Suetonius, snatched some bread out of his hand and then returned and gently replaced it.

Fig. 22

Lucumon settled in Rome, took the name of Tarquinius Priscus and was elected king. He reigned from 616 to 579 B.C. His old name, Lucumon, it may be noted, meant 'lord' or 'chieftain' in the Etruscan language. Once elected, Tarquin made various important innovations. He doubled the number of senators by introducing a hundred new members, who were given the title of 'second-class' *Patres* and who provided him with valuable support. It was his intention to swell the meagre ranks of Roman *equites* by creating new *centuriae*, but Attus Navius, a famous augur, opposed this on the grounds that the flight of the birds signified the gods' disfavour. Challenged by the angry king, the augur cut a stone with his razor, and this omen so increased the authority of omens and augurs generally that from that time nothing, either in internal politics or in affairs of war, was done without consulting them.

It was Tarquin who chose the site for the future *Circus Maximus*. He also instituted the Roman games or *Ludi Magni*, which took place there annually on the Ides of September. He set afoot a series of major undertakings, including the construction of a drainage system for the low-lying sector of Rome, a surrounding wall and foundations for a temple of

Jupiter on the Capitol. His successors, and in particular his son Tarquinius Superbus, developed and completed the works he began. Under his reign Rome undertook various military campaigns against the Sabines and Latins.

In the end Tarquin was assassinated by the sons of Ancus Marcius, who bore a grudge against the foreigner who had acquired powers which they considered rightfully their own. His wife, Tanaquil, installed Servius Tullius on the throne. This king, who reigned from 578 to 535 B.C., was the son either of a female slave or of a woman of note taken prisoner from the Latins. According to an ancient legend, he was engendered by the flames licking out of the fire in his home. Livy mentions only that his childhood was marked by amazing omens. Once, when he was asleep, a flame circled his head, but extinguished itself when he awoke. Servius's achievements were considerable. He was said to have established the scheme of class-division in the Roman constitution and initiated the city's census. The citizens were divided into five classes, subdivided into centuries; the first two classes, containing the wealthiest citizens, provided more than half the centuries, the other three provided a smaller number and the whole of the poorer part of the population was grouped in one century. All the various classes were liable for military duties, but the weapons required varied according to the wealth of the class concerned. Taken as a whole, the centuries made up a new assembly, the *comitia centuriata*, in which votes were cast by century and the majority was, of necessity, always on the side of the wealthy. The Servian system was, however, less aristocratic than that based on voting by *curiae*; the decision rested with fortune, not birth. The wealthy could elect whomever they liked to the magistracy.

Servius extended Rome's boundaries to include the Quirinal and the Viminal, divided the city into four territorial tribes and surrounded it with a strong continuous wall. He forced the Latins to join the Romans in building a temple to Diana on the Aventine. This was tantamount to declaring Rome's superiority over Latium. Tarquin the Elder's two sons who had married Servius's daughters hatched a conspiracy against him and assassinated him. Tullia, his own daughter, ordered her chariot to pass over his body.

Servius was succeeded by one of Tarquin the Elder's sons, Lucius Tarquinius, nicknamed Superbus (the Proud) on account of his conduct. He was to be the archetype of the tyrant. His power was founded on force alone and was never legitimized by the consent either of the people or of the Senate. To defend it, he used terror rather than popularity. He radically reduced the numbers of the Senate and even endeavoured to do without it altogether. He renewed the treaty with the Latins and formed mixed maniples of Romans and Latins. A good general, he succeeded in defeating the Volsci, a people renowned in battle, and took Gabii by a ruse. He then turned his attention to administration and successfully undertook various vast projects, building the tiers of the *Circus Maximus*, the *Cloaca Maxima* and a grandiose temple to Jupiter on the Capitol; this was intended to immortalize his reign. Certain omens which appeared during the early stages of the work on the sacred building foretold the future greatness of the *Urbs*.

While the first work was being done on the building, the gods signalled the future grandeur of the empire: the birds permitted the deconsecration of all the chapels except that of Terminus. The omen was interpreted in this way: Terminus stayed where he was; alone of all the gods he refused to be removed from his sacred ground; this was a sign of the solidity and stability of the whole state. This omen of durability was followed by another which announced the greatness of the Empire: it is said that while digging the foundations of the temple a human head was found with all the features in perfect condition. There could be no doubt that the discovery meant that this place would be at the head of the empire and of the world: thus spake all the soothsayers, both those of Rome and those who were brought from Etruria to study the question. (Livy, I, 55)

After sending a mission headed by his two sons to Delphi to consult the famous oracle on the subject of a disquieting omen, Tarquin prepared for war against the Rutuli. But one of his sons, Sextus Tarquinius, violated an honourable matron, Lucretia, who then killed herself after confessing her dishonour to her husband, Collatinus. This sparked off a revolutionary movement in Rome, which was already exasperated by the excesses of the royal family, and a Roman citizen, Lucius Junius Brutus, led an uprising to obtain liberty. He forced Tarquin, his wife and children to go into exile. By 509 the Roman Republic was born and the State passed into the hands of the Roman people, its rightful custodian. The *comitia cen turiata* elected two consuls, Lucius Junius Brutus and Lucius Tarquinius Collatinus. The monarchic régime in Rome had lasted two hundred and forty-four years.

This account of monarchic Rome mingles various elements, legendary accounts of different dates and provenance, Indo-European myths torn out of context and transformed into historical narratives, projections of later events and institutions into a more distant past and, finally, accurate memories of dates and cultural facts from a past still vivid in human memory. Until now we have been considering the origin and value of legends. We must go on to examine the emergence of culture on the site of Rome and the gradual progress of the newly founded town, with reference mainly to archaeology, taken in conjunction with textual evidence. First, however, some account of the geography of Latium and the Tiberine region must be given, for geographic conditions are always of immense importance in the study of the development and character of settlements.

CHAPTER IV

Latium and the Site of Rome

AT FIRST THE TERRITORY of the Latin people was
limited to the southern part of the lower valley of the
Tiber, a poorish region dominated by the Alban hills, on which
today stand the *castelli romani*. The flat coastline, without bays or
harbours, offered few possibilities of maritime activity or communication. To all intents and purposes the Tiber formed the
country's northern frontier, beyond which lay Etruria. However, the Falisci, a people ethnically related to the Latins, lived
on the right bank of the Tiber, north of Latium. From the
historic period onward their main towns were Falerii, Capena
and Narce. The political and cultural history of the Falisci,
surrounded as they were by the Etruscans, merges imperceptibly
with Etruscan history. Nevertheless their language, known to
us from various inscriptions, was of Latin origin although it
reveals numerous Sabine and Etruscan contaminations.

Close by, to the east of Latium were the foothills of the
Apennines, inhabited in the north by the Sabines, a simple,
uncouth tribe, and in the south by the Hernici. Latin
territory was later reduced still further by the arrival of the
Volsci between the Alban and Auruncan hills at the beginning
of historic times. They took over the ancient Latin cities of
Velletri, Segni, Satricum and Antium.

In comparison with the peninsula in general, which is
divided up into small areas by mountain ranges, the lower
valley of the Tiber has an important geographical advantage,
which has been often and justifiably stressed: it is a junction
for several natural thoroughfares. Two other regions of Italy
have the same advantage, though to a lesser degree: the central
stretch of the Arno valley, which gives access to various important Apennine passes and where Pistoia and Florence grew,

and the plain of Campania, which is within easy and convenient reach of the south. Several great natural routes converge on the plain of Latium and they were adopted, after the beginning of the historical period, by the main Roman roads, the *Via Appia*, running south along the coast, the *Via Latina* which led to Campania via the Sacco gap, the *Via Valeria*, following the course of the Aterno towards the Adriatic, the *Via Salaria*, which after following the course of the Tiber plunged into the mountains in the direction of Picenum and turned into the Ostian route along the coast of the Tyrrhenian sea, the *Via Aurelia*, bordering the sea towards the north. The *Via Cassia* crossed the Sabatine Hills, which were not very difficult to penetrate, and led to Etruria; the *Via Flaminia*, following the same route, also left Rome to the north but diverged after a short while to follow the valley of the Nera to Umbria and the Adriatic.

These Roman roads were based on older paths just as the network of modern highways has remained largely faithful to the lines laid down by the Roman road-builders. Thus Rome grew up in a region naturally endowed with easy and direct communications with the surrounding regions and in particular with the two provinces whose cultures were most advanced, Etruria and Magna Graecia. This factor doubtless constituted one of the main causes of Rome's amazing destiny.

The advantages of the site of Rome itself were recognized and enumerated as early as classical times. Cicero (*De republica*, II, 3-5), Livy (V, 54) and Strabo (V, 3, 7) all insist on the excellence of Rome's position, and the advantageous presence, in the form of the Tiber, of a great navigable river which gave swift access to both the sea and the centre of the peninsula. They were right; moreover, when Rome's size increased, the Tiber became a useful route for bringing both building materials and provisions to the capital from various parts of the world. Nevertheless, modern geographers choose to go more deeply into the matter and analyse the geographical factors which made Rome an eligible site in prehistoric times and no doubt influenced its foundation, long before they contributed to its rise to power. One of these factors is indeed the conver׳ gence of so many roads in Latium. But the site of Rome itself had certain very definite advantages.

The moderate׳sized Tiberine hills, caused by erosion, repre׳ sent the farther extremities of volcanic outflows from the Alban hills. Some of them, particularly the Palatine and the Capitol, had steep slopes which made them easy to defend. Certainly the Palatine's three crests, relatively large area and steep slopes made it the most suitable for early settlements, and it is not surprising that the first villages (of shepherds and herdsmen) were founded on it. The site did, however, put certain obstacles in the way of expansion; first the marshy nature of parts of it, necessitating a vast drainage system, and then the unevenness of the ground and the large number of small hills.

But this tightly knit group of *montes*, reaching almost to the river at the point opposite the only island in the Tiber in the whole area, made it easier to cross the Tiber at this level. The river itself flowed through a marshy, alluvial valley. The site of Rome thus formed a junction between the north and south of Latium and at the same time occupied a key position on the valley route along which salt was transported to the moun׳ tainous regions of the east. These features also favoured the construction of the first bridges across the Tiber above the river mouth. Farther downstream there was no suitable spanning place, and in fact the Roman bridges remained the lowest point at which the Tiber could be crossed until the nineteenth century. Consequently, the commercial and strategic advan׳ tages of the site were exceptional. With its bridges, its accessi׳ bility from the sea and its position as a road junction, the city had from the start supreme assets, which were to play an important part in the whole of its history.

Plates 19, 55
Fig. 4

THE SITE OF ROME:
ARCHAEOLOGY AND
FIRST HUMAN SETTLEMENTS

Plate 22

Fig. 4

Plates 23–41

With regard to the earliest times in Rome, the lack of literary sources and their questionable validity means that supreme importance attaches to archaeological evidence. It is the only reliable authority for any kind of assessment of the historical value of texts and hence the only thing which enables us to substitute factual history for legends. But the excavations of early Rome are of fairly recent date, and for a just appreciation of their results it is necessary to give some account of them.

The first important discoveries relative to archaic Rome—the Esquiline tombs and the sanctuaries and tombs of the Quirinal —were made in the last quarter of the nineteenth century. The great Esquiline cemetery was revealed during work on new building in the area. A useful work published by Pinza in 1905[1] collates this early evidence. The first organized, systematic excavations took place at the beginning of this century. Boni Vaglieri broke new and important ground, the former on the Palatine and in the Forum, the latter on the Palatine only. Using the most scrupulously scientific methods, Boni revealed the tombs of the vast *sepolcreto* in the Forum which are now preserved and exhibited exactly as they were found in the Antiquarium of the Forum. His writings on the subject were as precise and meticulous as his actual excavations. Vaglieri, on the Palatine, uncovered traces of primitive dwellings and a considerable amount of archaic material which is now collected together in the Antiquarium of the Palatine. But owing to the state of research at the time he was unable to appreciate the full significance of his own discoveries and there were many lively polemical exchanges between him and Pigorini. A large part of the material found in 1900–10 has remained

[1] See Bibliography, p. 155.

unpublished until the present day, although this is now being remedied.

Traces of archaic sanctuaries on the Capitol and at Sant' Omobono were discovered before the last war during impor⁄ tant excavations by M. A. Colini. Since 1945 the available material has been increased by a series of further discoveries. First there was the systematic research undertaken on the Palatine by eminent specialists of the Italian school: they provided vitally important information about the protohistory of the Palatine and material on which facts rather than hypotheses could be based. With regard to certain features of the Forum and the Palatine, recent discoveries have broadened our views as well as posing certain problems. Methodical researches are still being carried out along scrupulously scientific lines in various sectors of archaic Rome. The results to date are summed up in the en⁄ suing pages.[1]

THE BIRTH OF ROME AND EARLY DEVELOPMENTS IN THE SECOND HALF OF THE EIGHTH CENTURY B.C.

As a result of Boni's work at the beginning of the century and S. M. Puglisi's recent excavations, we now know of two very early dwelling sites situated next to one another on the two ridges of the Palatine, the Palatium and the Cermalus. Boni's excavations under the *domus Flaviorum* revealed in the lowest archaeological layer a complete series of post⁄holes together with pottery characteristic of the Early Iron Age, and wattle and daub. It is now clear that these are remains of prehistoric huts built on clay foundations. The latter had disappeared, but enough was left of the post⁄holes and the daub, which from Neolithic times was used to cover the walls of the huts made of thatch and branches, to prove the existence of Romulean⁄ period dwellings at about the middle of the eighth century B.C.

Fig. 4

[1] See p. 151 for developments since this book was first published.

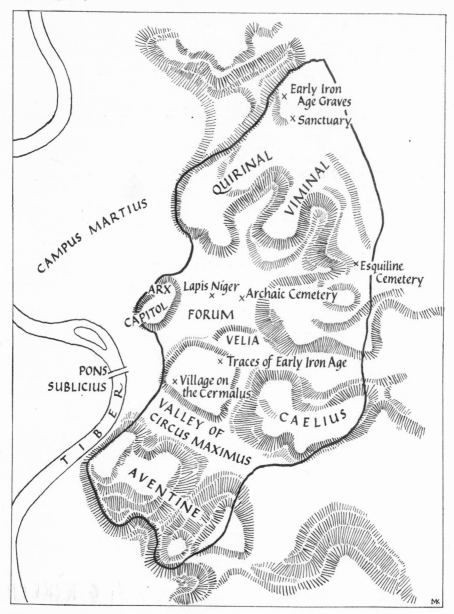

Fig. 4 *Excavations in archaic Rome. The black line indicates the site of the so-called Servian Wall*

Latin pottery, found in large quantities on various sites in the Alban hills and other parts of Latium, developed along lines parallel to those taken by Villanovan pottery as a whole; the only differences are simpler decoration, the frequency of

Fig. 5   Hut urn from Tarquinia

certain rather heavy and provincial vase-forms and of a charac-teristic cinerary urn, the hut urn, which are discussed below. The hut urn, however, can also be found in the Villanovan culture of Etruria, in cities such as Caere, Veii and Bisenzio. The oldest Latin culture thus appears to have been merely a regional variation, belated in many cases, of the two cultural phases in Etruria, known today as Villanovan I and advanced Villanovan, covering in the aggregate the years between 800

Fig. 5

and 700 B.C. The oldest material found in Rome, and in particular the pottery discovered among the hut foundations of the Palatium and under the *domus Flaviorum*, correspond with the material from the second phase in the Alban hills. Chronologically, then, the earliest objects discovered by Boni belong to the same period as late Villanovan material, i.e. about the middle of the eighth century B.C.

In 1907, D. Vaglieri discovered a series of channels dug into the tufa near the temple of Cybele. He himself misunderstood their function; they were in fact intended to carry away water from a sector of one of the protohistoric villages. It was in this part of the Cermalus that the *casa* or *tugurium Romuli*, a rustic hut, was piously preserved until the end of Roman antiquity. Trial excavations were undertaken in the same area in 1948, and the results of these were published in 1951. They revealed three hut bases, with much ceramic material, on the platform of tufa which forms the top of the hill at this point; the pottery was very similar to that found by Boni when excavating the Palatium. These foundations, here dug into the tufa on account of local geological conditions, are well preserved and give a clear picture of the general plan of the huts on the site. The depth of the foundations varies, but it always allows a large enough sill to protect the inside of the hut from flooding. Near this sill are holes in which, no doubt, stood the posts bearing the walls.

One set of foundations has been preserved in its entirety and is of cardinal interest; despite the very slight mutilations caused in the classical period, it is still possible to make out its details and characteristics. As with the other foundations, its plan is rectangular with gently rounded corners. A fairly large structure, measuring 13 feet 5 inches by 11 feet 9 inches, it is dug deep into the tufa, as can be seen from the sill surrounding it. On it was built a partly sunken dwelling, its floor being rather more than 1 foot 8 inches below the surrounding ground.

Plates 15, 16

Along the perimetral line are six main holes for the wooden posts which formed the solid framework for the walls. The diameter of these holes, 1 foot 3¾ inches at ground-level, decreases towards the bottom, and they are 1 foot 5¾ inches deep. Presumably the posts were held fast in the holes by means of stones and wooden wedges.

There is also a central hole with two others close by, at the point where the entrance is presumed to be; its function is explained by the funerary urns in hut form which have been found in large numbers in the Alban hills, in Rome itself and in many cities of Latium and southern Etruria. These urns are in the form of dwellings and represent an early but very precise funerary symbolism. They are made of clay, and the structural details of some of them have interested scholars for a long time; until very recently they were the only source of information regarding ancient Latin huts. Thanks to the discoveries on the Cermalus, however, these miniature huts can now be compared with ground plans of the real thing, and this has proved exceedingly instructive.

The central hole appears for the first time in the series of hut foundations scattered over Italy and originating in the Villano-van culture. There is nothing comparable in the hut foundations round Bologna, which are nevertheless sometimes as much as 16 feet in diameter. This peculiarity of the Palatine foundations accounts for the gabled roofs often found on hut urns. This type of roof seems to have been formed of a central ridge-piece from which side-beams branch out. The ridge-piece would have been a small *columen* shorter than the hut itself; this could not have rested vertically on the walls, which offered too little resistance. A central prop was needed to support both the *columen* and the roof in general. Its existence is confirmed by the central hole found in the hut foundations on the Palatine.

The entrance to the hut is clearly marked: on one of the short sides the external sill is lower for 3 feet 5¾ inches and

is stepped in tiers. This was the entrance, which was distinguished by curious details that can be explained architecturally.
On both sides in the interior of the hut were two holes,
$7\frac{7}{8}$ inches in diameter and $11\frac{3}{4}$ inches in depth. These mark
the position of the posts used as door-jambs; the door itself was
probably made of some primitive material covered with
branches and the groove running from jamb to jamb may be
taken to indicate its position. Corresponding with these
door-post holes there are outside the hut two other holes
of similar dimensions: $7\frac{7}{8}$ inches in diameter, $9\frac{7}{8}$ inches in
depth. These indicate the presence of a small porch in front of
the entrance, or an extension of the roof at this point. In
general, the roofs of the hut urns extended well beyond the
uprights of the walls; sometimes the extension is very pronounced. But it is not particularly accentuated in front of the
entrance opening. Its function is to protect the walls from water
running down from the roof. An urn from Campo Fattore,
now in the Pigorini Prehistoric Museum, Rome, is constructed
in a special way that recalls the Palatine huts. Outside, on
either side of the door, two double supports, made of large
tree-trunks, bear the weight of the edge of the roof. In other
hut urns the ribs, incorporated into the walls themselves, frame
the entrance to the dwelling: this is the case with the Urn of
Tarquinia, which is also in the Pigorini Prehistoric Museum
(numbered in the catalogue as 85.689).

Another curious structural analogy must be mentioned. On
the north-west side of the Palatine hut a gap in the outside sill
marks the position of a lateral opening 2 feet $3\frac{5}{8}$ inches broad
—a feature also found in certain urns from Latium. In exactly
the same way an urn from Castel Gandolfo, now in the
Pigorini Prehistoric Museum in Rome, and another from
Tarquinia, in the municipal museum, have lateral openings
with their bases on a level with the base of the door. It seems
likely, therefore, that the most advanced dwellings of Latium

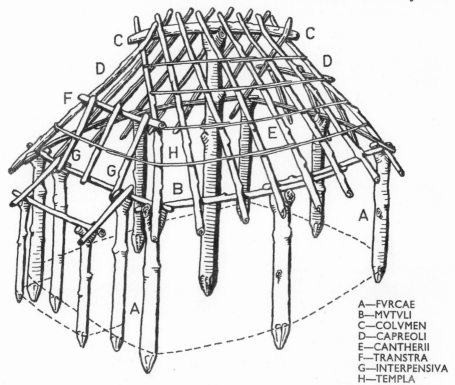

A—FVRCAE
B—MVTVLI
C—COLVMEN
D—CAPREOLI
E—CANTHERII
F—TRANSTRA
G—INTERPENSIVA
H—TEMPLA

Fig. 6   Wooden reconstruction by A. Davico of the largest of the huts whose foundations have been found on the Palatine. Antiquarium of the Palatine

in the Early Iron Age had a side window; if it was seldom represented in the hut urns, this was because of the need to simplify when modelling a clay vessel. Whenever it appears, the side window is the only one in the building and in exactly the same position as in the Palatine example. Its function was to give light to the back of the hut; it may also have served as a handy chute for the ejection of domestic refuse. Two furrows in the tufa of the Palatine do, in fact, lead down to the outside of the hut and eventually to a drainage channel.

These few examples show the amount of information about the dwellings of the Early Iron Age to be extracted from the new discoveries and the extent to which they correspond, even in detail, with the architecture of the hut urns. From this informa-tion it was possible to reconstruct a faithful, if small-scale,

Fig. 6
Plates 17, 18

model of the primitive hut, clearly showing the actual frame-work of the structure. Now in the Antiquarium of the Palatine, it gives some idea of the degree of precision reached by archae-ological analysis. The position of the posts or supports (*furcae*) was determined by reference to the position of the perimetral holes. The ends of these supports were bridged by horizontal beams (*mutuli*) which strengthened them and also acted as supports for the transverse elements of the roofing (*cantherii*). The latter rested on the ridge-pole or *columen*, whose central post took the weight. The ends of the *columen* rested on the *capreoli*, which in their turn rested on the forked ends of the outside supporting posts. The details of the roof are taken from the information provided by hut urns. The upper ends of the *cantherii*, which joined in the form of a cross at the highest point of the roof, were protected by a clay covering in the form of a figurative model, often representing birds. Horizontal beams or *templa* rested on the *cantherii* at different levels. This basic roof-structure, like the walls, was covered with branches and thatch laid over a coating of dried clay. Fragments of this coating bearing the marks of the branches which pressed on it were found during excavation. These are the primitive walls referred to by Ovid: *'paries lento vimine textus'* (*Fasti*, VI, 262).

By means of excavation it has been possible to reach the oldest archaeological layer which would correspond with the period when the hut was actually in use. The layer is 8 inches deep and comprises many fragments of pottery belonging to the Early Iron Age. Details of the domestic life led in the hut were gleaned from remains of a hearth, in which there were ash and charcoal, in the middle of the dwelling, not far from the hole for the central post. Remains of an earthenware furnace characteristic of the period were also found, as well as many fragments of household utensils scorched by the fire or bearing traces of black smoke-marks. Pieces of charred animal bones represented the remains of meals taken in the hut. It is hard to tell how long the Palatine dwelling was used, although, judging by the small depth of the lower stratum, it seems likely that it was limited to two or three generations.

As already mentioned, few excavations have yielded so much and such precise information about archaic Rome. We have concentrated on the earliest way of life illustrated by the Palatine hut, that which belongs to the second half of the eighth century. But life did of course continue on the site, and by means of the superimposed strata it is possible to follow the cultural progress step by step. The period corresponding with the seventh century will be dealt with later on.

But first we must consider what happened in the earliest, or Romulean, period in other parts of the Roman site. In theory it should be possible, by means of excavation, to distinguish all the different forms of settlements either by unearthing the dwellings themselves or by identifying the cemeteries belonging to them. But the earth disturbances of nearly three thousand

Fig. 7 Cremation grave Y of the Forum cemetery. Section of its small well and dolium *showing the objects as they were found when the grave was opened. Mean height of* dolium *1 ft. 10½ in.*

Fig. 8 Cremation grave Y. The dolium, *but urn and various votive objects among which may be noted the reticulated vases and the fibula* ad arco serpeggiante. *Second half of the eighth century. cf. Fig. 7*

years and the presence of the modern city put a total survey out of the question. The most that can be hoped for is a certain amount of fragmentary evidence, which increases only very gradually.

The systematic excavations that have been going on for some fifty years have revealed a fairly extensive cemetery in the Forum; a large number of its graves date back to the Early Iron Age and are contemporary with the Palatine hut. South-east of the temple of Antoninus and Faustina, in the narrow area not damaged by later buildings, Boni unearthed about forty graves; their plan was most carefully noted and the material scrupulously collected. Finally, the graves were reconstructed in the Antiquarium of the Forum where it is now possible to study them in comfort. The graves are of two types: for crema-tion and for inhumation. The former were pits, at the bottom of which was placed the *dolium* which was closed with a lid.

Plates 20, 23-27

Plates 26, 37, 41

Figs. 7, 8, 10

The *dolium* contained the cinerary vase, often a hut urn, and several small votive jars. The inhumation graves, twenty seven in number, were *fossae* in which the body was often stretched out in an oak coffin. With one exception, these graves contained no hut urns, but the rest of their material resembled that of the cremation graves—biconical urns, goblets with reticulated ornamentation, twohandled cups and bossed am phorae. In several cases the *fossa*graves cut into and link up with the pitgraves.

Plates 28, 29, 32,
34, 36, 37, 38
Fig. 9

Plates 24–26

Any historical interpretation of the *sepolcreto* is bound to depend to a large extent on the precise dating of the various graves; this is a difficult problem, but scholars are attempting to solve it by devoting close attention to the votive objects discovered. We have room here for only a broad outline of the results obtained; a recent valuable book[1] has analysed the material grave by grave. The oldest graves, both pit and *fossa*, date back to the Early Iron Age and extend into the second half of the eighth century. They are thus contemporary with the Palatine hut. Everything points to the fact that the occupants of the huts on the Cermalus and Palatium buried their dead in this part of the Forum valley, which was only about 350 feet away from their dwellingplaces. The Velia, a low hill, gave easy access from the Palatine village to the *sepolcreto*, which must therefore be assumed to be the burial place of the first occupants of the Palatine huts.

However, the oldest Forum grave, discovered during recent excavations, was at some distance from the *sepolcreto*, near the Arch of Augustus. This was a cremation grave;[2] the material found indicates that it is slightly older than the oldest graves found by Boni, and up to the present it remains an isolated example. Probably this separate grave was made at a time

[1] See Bibliography, p. 156 (Gjerstad, E.).
[2] See the article by S. M. Puglisi in *Bollettino di Paletnologia Italiana*, VIII, Part 4, 1951–52, pp. 45 sqq.

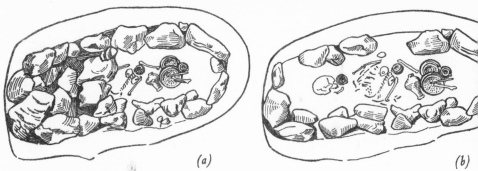

(a) *(b)*

Fig. 9 *Inhumation grave P of the Forum cemetery. Views of the grave with its covering of stones (a); without this covering (b).*

before there was any organized village on the Palatine. When the village emerged, however, it created the cemetery exca/ vated by Boni, whose chronological phases run parallel with its own.

But in March 1954 an archaic cremation grave was dis/ covered which dates from approximately the middle of the eighth century B.C. It is situated on the Palatine, behind the house of Livia, about half/way between the two hut/groups on the Cermalus and Palatium.[1] In it were found a *dolium* with a lid, a small clay stove, *olle* in a smooth *impasto* and another *olla* covered with plastic decoration in reticulated form, and a curved bronze fibula, all of which can be placed in the middle of the eighth century; the tomb is, therefore, contemporary with the Palatine dwellings. This is surprising, because from the outset the religious custom in Rome, as in the rest of Latium, was to bury the dead in a common burial/place at some distance from the dwelling/places of living people. The only people buried near the huts were children or babies, who were sometimes placed in earthenware jars under the roof/extension: a child's grave from the end of the sixth century was discovered

[1] See the article by G. Carettoni, 'Tomba arcaica a cremazione, scoperta sul Palatino' in *Bollettino di Paletnologia Italiana*, IX, 1954–55, pp. 261 sqq.

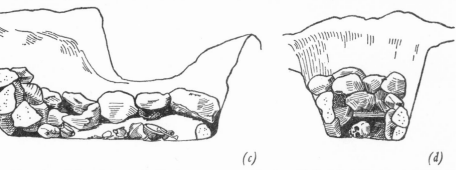

(c)   *(d)*

Fig. 9 (contd.) Lengthways section (c); transverse section (d). Second half of the eighth century. cf. Pl. 34, 36, 37. For dimensions, see Note to Plate 36, p. 202.

in 1950 on the Palatine beneath the *aula regia* of the palace of the Flavians (*see Antichità*, II, 1950, p. 1, 599). But the cremation grave of the house of Livia did not contain a child, and one can only resort to hypothetical explanations. As far as our present documentation goes, it appears to be an exceptional occurrence: at the time of the first occupation of the Cermalus and Palatium, it was possible to bury a corpse in a still isolated spot at some distance from the dwellings themselves.

On the other hand, there are two funerary groups whose oldest parts also date back to the second half of the eighth century, namely, the Esquiline and Quirinal cemeteries, which were first excavated in 1870. Although an inventory was made of the contents, the relevant research was, even for the period, unsystematic, and it is not now always easy to interpret. A fairly extensive cemetery was found on the Oppius, one of the spurs of the Esquiline. Most of the graves were for inhumation, as can be seen from their contents. But four cremation graves were also found, with a hut urn and three ossuaries bearing traces of burning. The part of this cemetery richest in remains, which was found in the region of the *Via G. Lanza* and the *Via Merulana*, dates only from the late seventh century, but the oldest cremation graves and some of the *fossa*-graves

Fig. 4

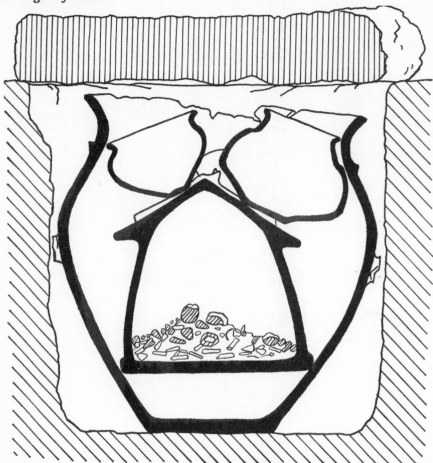

Fig. 10   Cremation grave GG of the Forum cemetery. Section of the pozzetto, dolium, *and its contents. Second half of the eighth century. Height of* dolium *1 ft. 3¾ in., max. diameter 1 ft. 2¼ in.*

date back to the Early Iron Age and can be assigned to the last decades of the eighth century. No dwellings have been found on the Esquiline, although there is reason to think that dwellings existed on it from the Early Iron Age, very shortly after the beginning of the Palatine village.

Finally, five inhumations, discovered in the last century on the Quirinal, near Santa Susanna, date from the same period. Although they are few in number, they lead to the inference that there were contemporary dwellings on the Quirinal hill.

This is what archaeology tells us about the period which was occupied, according to traditional Roman history, by Romulus's reign and the beginning of that of Numa Pompilius. The interpretation of this evidence which has now been avail/ able for some time has led to much discussion in scholarly circles, which still continues. The existence of two different funerary rites—cremation, which prevailed in the earliest phase of the *sepolcreto* of the Forum, and inhumation, which soon predominated in the graves in the Esquiline cemetery and is the only rite evidenced in the Quirinal graves—seemed to point to a confirmation of the two peoples of the traditional story who shared the Roman site from Romulus's times. It also led to the theory that Latin tribes who burned their dead built a certain number of dwellings on the ridges of the Palatine and also, no doubt, before their final departure, on the Esquiline; but at about the same time Sabine tribes, on whom the annals laid significant stress, entered the site from the north, having taken the salt/route. Reaching the spur of the Quirinal, they settled on it and on the Capitol, and were thus separated from the Latin settlements by the marshy valley of the Forum. They then spread on to the Esquiline, which would account for the rapid predominance of the rite of burial in the large cemetery on the Oppius.

Excellent scholars, such as Signor S. M. Puglisi, tend nowa/ days to adduce less exclusively ethnic reasons for the duality of funerary rites attested by archaeological finds than heretofore. On the one side Latium bordered on a region where the Villanovan culture was developing (i.e. southern maritime Etruria); on the other side it bordered on a region characterized by its Subappenine culture (i.e. the Osco/Umbrian area).

Plates 33, 35
Figs. 7, 8, 10
Plates 28–32, 34
Fig. 9

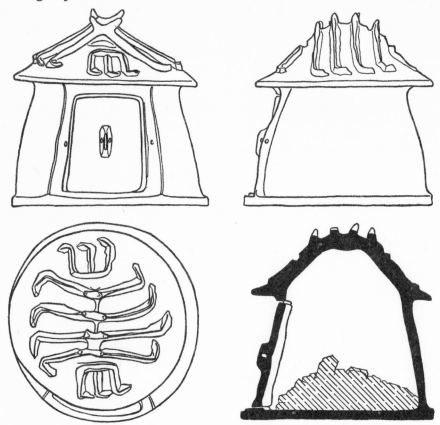

Fig. 11 Hut urn from grave GG of the Forum cemetery. Diameter of base 9⅞ in., total height 10 1/16 in.

These two factors could account for the arrival in Rome of different cultural influences and the coexistence there of the rite of inhumation (coming from the Osco-Umbrian area) and the rite of cremation (coming from southern Etruria).

This disposes of the traditional hypothesis according to which peoples of different origins were living on the site of Rome from its very beginnings. Cultural influences from different areas would suffice to explain the existence side by side of inhumation

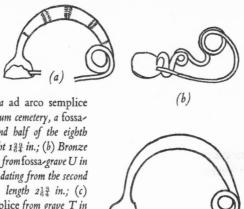

Fig. 12 (*a*) *Bronze fibula* ad arco semplice
*from grave KK of the Forum cemetery, a fossa-
grave dating from the second half of the eighth
century: length* 2⅓¾ *in., height* 1⅓¾ *in.; (b) Bronze
fibula* ad arco serpeggiante *from* fossa-grave U *in
the Forum cemetery, a grave dating from the second
half of the eighth century: length* 2⅓¾ *in.; (c)
Bronze fibula* ad arco semplice *from grave T in
the Forum cemetery, a* pozzo-grave *dating from
the second half of the eighth century: length* 2⅝ *in.,
height* 1⅛ *in.*

and cremation in the oldest Roman tombs. It is true that the
meagre and fragmentary information provided by archaeology is
insufficient to reconstruct a precise and detailed history of this
first phase of Roman life. However, there seems to be enough
agreement between the epic classical accounts and the information provided by archaeological excavations to support, in
general, the idea of the presence of two different peoples, Latin
and Sabine, in early Rome. The presence of different cultures
on the different hills seems to be proved by the persistence in
the historical period of ancient religious ceremonies which point
to a stage when the population was made up of isolated hill
settlements. The ritual race of the Luperci round the Palatine
on February 15 represented a magic rite for the defence of the
oldest Roman settlement. Recently, attempts have been made
to pin-point specific religious survivals recalling a Sabine settlement on the *colles* in the north of Rome which existed
alongside a Latin people in the *montes* beyond the Forum.
Such survivals were few, and it is often difficult to classify them
owing to our doubts about the original character, Italic or

Latin, of this or that cult or divinity. Taken in conjunction with the dedication of the Palatine to the god Pales, the dedication of the Quirinal to Quirinus, god of the assembly (*quirites*), seems significant. There is too much support, from varying sources, for the traditional view unanimously accepted by the Ancients, for it to be wholly discounted.

The cultural level of Rome in the eighth century can only be deduced by examining the contents of the dwellings and cemeteries. This material is of a good standard, similar in every way to what has been found in the cemeteries in the Alban hills, but often better finished. The contents of the oldest graves on the Forum and Esquiline indicate that the first Roman dwellings had attained a certain wealth, however relative. There are, for instance, numerous bronze objects, fibulae in particular. It seems, therefore, that the Rome of the eighth century could well stand comparison with the many Iron Age settlements scattered over the plain of Latium.

Figs. 8, 12

CHAPTER V

Rome from about 700 to the Beginning of the Fifth Century B.C.

B Y STUDYING the archaeological discoveries in the different parts of archaic Rome along strictly topographical lines, it is possible to make out a slow but continuous progression in Roman culture from about 700 to 550 B.C. This timedivision is justifiable, for after the first part of the sixth century the life of Rome takes on a different appearance and the collection of more or less united villages gives place to a prosperous town worthy of the name. But until this time the progress of Roman culture was far less rapid than the traditional story would have us believe.

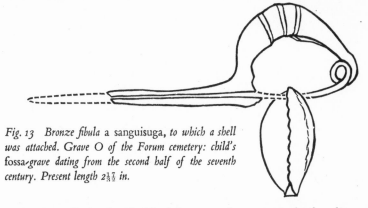

Fig. 13   Bronze fibula a sanguisuga, *to which a shell was attached. Grave O of the Forum cemetery: child's fossagrave dating from the second half of the seventh century. Present length 2¾ in.*

As regards the first half of the seventh century, the localization of remains found indicates that the settlements were not very extensive. Although the Latin settlements continued an active existence, as can be seen from the archaeological layer corresponding with the period to which Italian prehistorians have given the name of 'the Second Iron Age', it is surprising to find that there were fewer graves in the *sepolcreto* of the Forum.

85

Not until the second half of the seventh century did burial, places increase again, though at that stage the dead were buried inside tree-trunks. On the other hand, recent important excava, tions in a region not far from the Forum, near the Arch of Augustus, have revealed three cremation graves for adults and five children's graves or *suggrundaria*.[1]

Chronologically, the adult graves come midway between the two main series of *sepolcreto* graves and date from about the middle of the seventh century, filling in a curious gap in the use of the Forum valley for funerary purposes. But the question of the settlements to which these new graves belonged remains open, for their culture, as illustrated by the material found, seems to differ slightly from that of the *sepolcreto* and shows affinities with an archaic Villanovan culture found in a group of graves on the La Tolfa hills. Does this indicate an influx of people from the Allumiere-La Tolfa region? It is impossible to say. Often, we have seen, new discoveries pose more problems than they solve; of necessity the progress of knowledge in a matter as complex as this is slow and difficult.

New excavations confirm that in the seventh century the Forum was not only used for burial but also inhabited in certain parts. They have revealed traces of hut-foundations with holes for post-supports between the temple of Julius and the Arch of Augustus. According to E. Gjerstad these date from the period following the years 670–660; floods destroyed the lowest inhabited zone shortly before 625 B.C. At first the settle, ment was restricted to its upper portion; then, after the installa, tion of a drainage system foreshadowing the public works of the Etruscan kings, the whole of the zone was again occupied by huts from roughly 625 to 575 B.C. The drainage system allowed the settlement to extend as far as the lowest part of the Forum valley, as can be seen from the remains of huts of this

[1] See S. M. Puglisi, 'Sepolcri di incinerati nella valle del Foro romano' in *Bollettino di Paletnologia Italiana*, IX, 1954–55, pp. 300 sqq.

Fig. 14 Ovoid proto-corinthian aryballos, found among the votive objects in grave G of the Forum cemetery. Grave G is that of a child about a year old buried in the trunk of an oak tree. Evidence as to date is given by the aryballos, which belongs to about 650 B.C. Height $2\frac{9}{16}$ in., lip diameter $1\frac{1}{8}$ in. cf. Pl. 40

period found during excavations on the site of the *Equus Domitiani*. In about 575 B.C., the age of huts came to an end, and soon rapid developments in all fields were to give a decisive impetus to the emergence of Rome proper.

During the seventh century the Esquiline cemetery con⁄tinued to be used and even, it seems, to increase in size, so far as we can judge from the evidence of early excavations. The contents of the graves increase along parallel lines with that of the *sepolcreto* graves. First, there are painted urns with geometri⁄cal decoration, then Faliscan objects and the first appearance of the *bucchero*. In the second half of the seventh century, late proto⁄Corinthian urns appeared; they form part of the contents of a chamber⁄tomb which was probably used many times.

Outside these areas, finds dating back to the first half of the seventh century are sporadic, and insufficient for any firm conclusions. In the second half of the century the position changes. Traces of sanctuaries appear in the northern part of Rome, although there are no surviving architectural remains of the temples themselves. Their presence can, however, be in⁄ferred from the *favissae* or votive stores, originally situated alongside the sacred buildings themselves, whose contents have been found. A very productive *favissa* has been located at the northern extremity of the Quirinal, not far from the spot where the *fossa*⁄graves of the eighth century were found. The material seems to extend over the whole of the seventh century and the beginning of the next. There are several *bucchero* vases dating from the period 650–580, as well as painted Italo⁄Corinthian vases. Another *favissa* was discovered last century in front of the Palace of the Quirinal, but little is known about it. It is now almost impossible to date it.

The discoveries made on the Capitol are also important for this period. A pit surrounded by blocks of a tufa called *cappel⁄laccio* was found between the temple of Jupiter on the Capitol and the church of Santa Maria dell' Aracoeli. Both its *bucchero* vases and those imitating the Corinthian style belong to about 600. The sanctuary indicated by this *favissa* must, therefore, have been older than the Etruscan temple of the Tarquins, and its disappearance was perhaps due to the work necessitated by the Etruscans' vast building projects. Shortly before the last war, remains of two temples, architectonic debris and many fragments of different vases were found at the foot of the Capitol, at the end of the small plain of the Forum Boarium, close by the church of Sant'Omobono. The pottery objects include embossed or undecorated *bucchero* ware, painted vases on Corinthian models and many Attic vases. Their dates range from the beginning to the end of the sixth century. It would seem, therefore, that the temples of Sant'Omobono were in use from about 600 to near the end of the Etruscan period.

In addition, various isolated, sporadic finds have revealed a body of material, mostly pottery, from different parts of the Forum and Palatine. As far as the first half of the seventh century is concerned, the number of objects of Faliscan origin or inspiration is striking. The material for the second half of the seventh century and the beginning of the sixth is considerably greater. Etruscan work is represented by a large number of *bucchero* vases in different forms, above all *oinochoai*, chalices and *kantharoi*. In various places fragments of painted Italo-Corin-thian fragments have been found. Finally, Greek importations are evidenced by the presence of Ionic and Attic vases, the former dating from the end of the seventh, the latter from the first half of the sixth century.

What conclusions can be legitimately drawn from this neces-sarily fragmentary and incomplete evidence which, nevertheless, in the aggregate constitutes an impressive body of fact? Let us make a distinction between the topographical and cultural fields. Until about the middle of the seventh century there seems to have been little modification of the villages which had developed earlier; on the other hand, it is now realized that from about 670 the Forum, which had until then been used only as a burial ground, came to be used for dwellings, for a hut village, in fact. Then, from 650, both sacred and secular life developed considerably on the northern hills, the Quirinal, Viminal and Capitol, and also in the region of the Forum Boarium bordering the Tiber. A yearly religious ceremony celebrated in the classical period in Rome and mentioned in many texts, the feast of the *Septimontium*, looked back in fact to a very early Roman federation which included only the villages that were by tradition Latin. On December 11 an archaic type of ceremony was celebrated by the peoples of the seven Latin hills: the three eminences of the Palatine, Cermalus, Palatium and Velia; the three eminences of the Esquiline, Fagutal, Cispius and Oppius; and, lastly, Caelius (some texts add Subura, which was situated between Oppius and Cispius). They offered up seven separate sacrifices, recalling an ancient union between the different *montes*. The Quirinal, Viminal and Capitol in the north and the Aventine in the south were excluded from this first federation. So also were the valleys of the Forum and *Circus Maximus*.

It is difficult to give a precise date to the time when this federation was first formed. The absence of the Forum, which was inhabited from 670 to 660, suggests that it occurred very early, probably in the first quarter of the seventh century. Apart from archaeological evidence, the most conclusive proof of different stages of topographical development in Rome is provided by certain very ancient rites in the Roman religion.

By studying the archaeological evidence it is possible to reach a fairly exact idea of the level of culture reached by the city in the period under consideration. Until about 650 B.C. Rome presents the appearance of a small Latin town, very different from the wealthy towns of Etruria or Praeneste, but not com/ pletely self-contained. Like most of its neighbours in Latium it

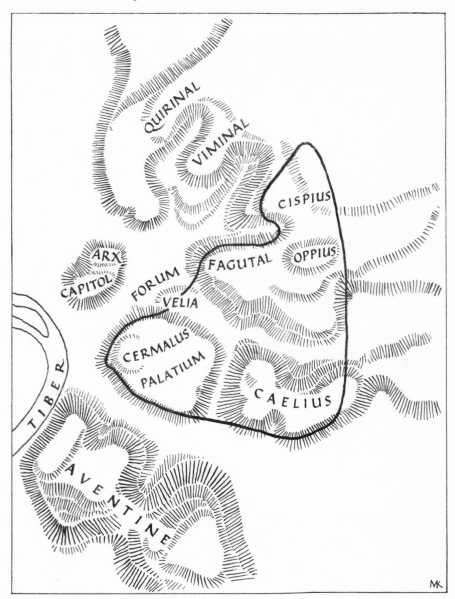

Fig. 15   The hills of Rome and the limits of the Septimontium

maintained constant commercial relations with the Falerians and Faliscan territory, as can be seen from the large quantity of Faliscan or Faliscan-inspired pottery found on its site. It was a town of merchants and workmen as well as of small farmers and stock-breeders.

Plates 43–5

In the next century Rome continued to grow and develop her intercourse with the countries north of the Tiber, the Faliscan area and southern Etruria. We have already remarked on the presence of many vases imported from the neighbouring lucumony of Caere. The Etruscan *bucchero* style reveals that the links between Rome and Etruscan territory were already close. But Rome was still a long way from the wealth and power of her Etruscan neighbours, such as Veii and Caere. The hut age continued until about 575, and shortly afterwards this long period of slow progression came to an end. Thus the conquests and foreign expansion attributed by classical historians to Rome in the seventh century are anachronisms; the inhabitants of the seven hills were certainly not in a position to destroy Alba or to found on the mouth of the Tiber a port which is, in any case, several centuries later in date. But now Rome's slow evolution was suddenly to speed up. The city leapt in one bound to greatness and prosperity.

ETRUSCAN ROME:
FROM ABOUT 550 TO ABOUT 475 B.C.

Fig. 15

This period is well documented by archaeological evidence. It is provided not by the cemeteries which have by now practically disappeared, but by numerous objects of different kinds, found mainly on the Forum and Palatine and including for the first time important traces of monuments, drains, walls and temples. Large quantities of Attic pottery with black-figure decoration have been found in Sant'Omobono and on the Forum and Palatine; the fragments are often of a very high quality and date from 550 to 500 B.C. This type of painted vase

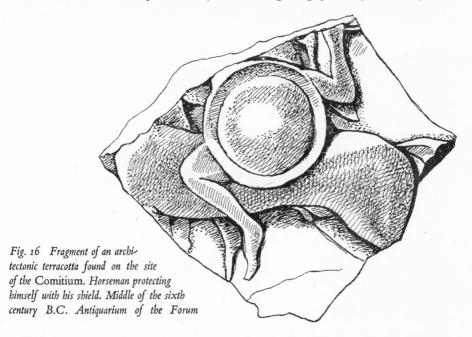

Fig. 16   Fragment of an archi-tectonic terracotta found on the site of the Comitium. *Horseman protecting himself with his shield. Middle of the sixth century B.C. Antiquarium of the Forum*

is followed in the first quarter of the fifth century by many fragments of Attic cups with red-figure decoration. Then, in about 480, the importation of Greek pottery to Rome seems almost to have ceased.

Beautiful polychrome terracottas, similar to original objects from other cities in Latium and Etruria, appear in various places, on the Capitol, the Palatine, the Esquiline, the Forum Romanum and the Forum Boarium. The terracottas in ques-tion are antefixes or fragments of friezes, proving the existence, on all the sites where they have been found, of richly decorated sacred buildings. According to tradition, it was Tarquin who completed the vast temple on the Capitol dedicated to Jupiter, Juno and Minerva. He devised a tripartite plan as appropriate to three divinities: Jupiter occupied the central *cella*, Juno and Minerva the two side *cellae*. The sanctuary thus had the

Figs. 16, 17
Plates 46, 47,
50, 51

93

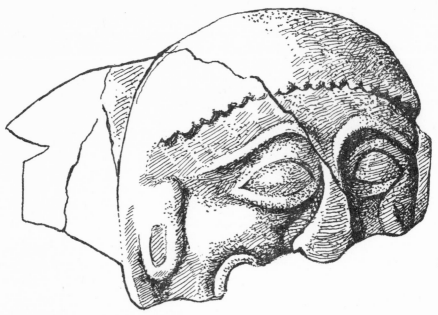

Fig. 17 Fragment of a terracotta antefix found in the Roman Forum on the site of the Lapis Niger. *Second half of the sixth century B.C. Antiquarium of the Forum*

appearance of an Etruscan temple, as in Vitruvius's detailed description (IV, 61); similar temples can be seen in many Etruscan cities. Only the base was of stone, the superstructure being of wood and the decoration and facings of terracotta. Now important traces of a powerful sub-foundation have been found on the Capitol, along with fragments of antefixes dating from the end of the sixth century. These are without any doubt the remains of the famous Capitoline temple. Other vestiges of the building work of the Tarquins still exist. There are, for instance, the remains of the *Cloaca Maxima*, which drained the marshy land of the Forum. Of the walls built round Rome at different periods there remain a certain number of sections, about which there has been much scholarly disagreement; it is

Fig. 18

not easy to assign a definite date to these archaic walls, since the same types of construction often persisted for centuries. In my opinion, however, only one conclusion can be drawn from the ground/plans of protective walls built according to the tech/ nique of the *opera quadrata*, in which blocks of stone in the shape of parallelepipeds were juxtaposed and superimposed on one another without any mortar. The walls made of *capellaccio*, a sort of grey tufa, date back to the Etruscan kings and represent the work attributed, by tradition, to King Servius. The wall in *grotta oscura*, a yellowish tufa quarried near Veii, is much later; it dates from after the capture of Rome by the Gauls in 390 and represents a defence reaction by the city, which had not yet recovered from the terrors of the barbarian invasion.

Plate 14

Figs. 4, 18

Thus Rome was a large city surrounded by a protective wall more than six miles long; the stranger entering the Tarquins' city would see a powerful line of fortifications and the rather massive, multi/coloured bulk of the many sanctuaries on the

Fig. 18   Part of the enclosing wall known as the 'Servian Wall' built by means of the technique called opera quadrata. *These remains are situated close to the station at Rome*

95

hills. So far, archaeology supports the traditional story; the historian can thus devote his attention to clarifying important questions of chronology and culture.

According to tradition, it will be remembered, Rome fell into the hands of the Etruscan kings 138 years after its founda/ tion by Romulus; in 616, according to Varro's calculations. Etruscan domination lasted a little more than a hundred years and ended in 509 with the expulsion of the hated tyrant. In fact, as we have seen, though Etruscan influence was of very early date, the actual presence of Etruscans and the transforma/ tion of Rome into a large city comparable with the lucumonies of southern Tuscany dates back only to about 550. The Tuscan annexation of the town on the banks of the Tiber must, therefore, be post/dated by half a century. In my opinion, archaeology does not warrant an earlier date and, inversely, a chronology which places the beginning of the Tyrrhenian monarchy at the end of the sixth century does not seem to me to be acceptable. When did the Etruscans finally leave Rome? According to the same basic chronology, it could only have been in about 450 B.C., more than fifty years after the traditional date. This also seems hard to believe. First of all, the later the period, the more chance there is of the traditional dates being correct. Nor does archaeology seem to support this view. It is true that Attic pottery continued to be imported during the first quarter of the fifth century, and the fragments of high/quality vessels with red/figure decoration date from the years between 500 and 480. But imported Attic pottery became extremely rare in the following period, a sure sign of impoverishment and a lower economic level. The architectonic terracottas also dis/ appeared. It is clear that this very obvious change marks the departure of the Etruscans and the return of Rome to the status of a Latin city, abandoned by its powerful invaders and beset by all kinds of difficulties.

The period from 509 to about 475 remains doubtful. Even

the traditional account is rather confused and seems to be intended mainly as a sop to Roman pride. In outline it states that Tarquinius Superbus left with his two sons for Caere after his people had rebelled against him. Seeking revenge, he raised two armies, one at Veii, the other at Tarquinia, and marched on Rome. But the Roman army, led by the two consuls, Junius Brutus and P. Valerius (Tarquinius Collatinus, Brutus's one/ time colleague had been exiled in accordance with the decree of banishment against the whole of the Tarquin family), scattered the Etruscans. The Tarquins then took refuge with Porsenna in the great city of Clusium. Porsenna, taking their part, marched on Rome at the head of a large army. He took possession of the Janiculum and was making ready to penetrate into Rome itself by means of a wooden bridge when he was halted by the heroism of Horatius Cocles. C. Mucius Scaevola attempted to kill the Etruscan king, was stopped by his guards, and to show his scorn of pain, placed his right hand in the flames. Porsenna, moved by this show of courage, agreed to conclude a peace treaty with Rome.

He then led his expeditionary force against the Latin town of Aricia to whose aid came the surrounding Latin peoples and the Greeks of Cumae. The soldiers of Aricia were dis/ persed, but those of Cumae surrounded the Tuscan army and decimated it. So ended Porsenna's expedition.

But in another version he does not retreat peaceably from before the walls of Rome. The assault is made and the town taken (Tacitus, *Histories*, III, 72). The impression gained from these accounts is that Rome, far from having taken the lead in these dramatic events, was merely a pawn in struggles between greater powers. From the third decade of the fifth century B.C., Etruria was beset by difficulties on all sides. On land her links with Campania were broken by the loss of Latium. On sea Cumae took the initiative and with the help of Syracusan ships, defeated her in 474—a defeat pregnant with consequences which marked the end of her supremacy in the Tyrrhenian sea. Thus, underneath the padding of the traditional story a framework of fact can be perceived. It was, no doubt, the alliance between the Latin towns—all of which were hostile to the Etruscans—and the Greeks of Cumae that drove them out of Rome and Latium as a whole. But beforehand, the Etruscan chiefs must have put up a stubborn resistance to their enemies. The Tarquins did not succumb to a mere internal revolt but to the combined forces of several enemies. And if Rome was in fact reconquered, even though only briefly, by the armies of the distant lucumony of Clusium, it shows the importance attached by the Tuscans to this key position on the Tiber. It was only lack of unity that prevented the various Etruscan towns from resisting the Greek-Latin alliance for a longer period.

The drama that was to decide the future of the Etruscan empire and, as a consequence, of Rome was played out in the last years of the sixth and the first quarter of the fifth century. This period saw the departure of the Tarquins from Rome, then the temporary reconquest of the city by allied Etruscan chiefs. Archaeology does not indicate cultural changes until about 475 B.C. Whatever the validity of the traditional date, 509, it was only after the first quarter of the fifth century that Rome became a small Latin city once again and Tyrrhenian luxury and splendour disappeared for good. Other records, to which we shall return later, confirm this first impression. In my opinion there is one kind of remembered facts—religious facts —which stands an unusually good chance of having been preserved with accuracy and exactitude in the Roman memory. The weight of religious tradition and the temple archives allow almost no doubt as to the fidelity of such recollections. Partisan feelings and the distorting influence of the *gentes'* pride only contrived to modify the details of these accounts, not their substance. Now, the number and kind of cults which appeared in Rome between 509 and 475 B.C. are very revealing. The great temple of the Capitoline Triad was consecrated in 509, that of Saturn, an ancient Italic deity, in 496; that of Ceres, Plate 56 Liber and Libera in 493. Mercury, god of trade, was built a temple near the Porta Capena in 495 and in 484 the Dioscuri installed themselves in their temple on the Forum. This is an impressive series of buildings. During the whole of the rest of the century we know of the founding of only two temples, that of Dius Fidius in 466, and that of Apollo in 431. It is hard to imagine that so many sanctuaries would have been built in this short period and with such costly decorations, one at least executed under the direction of great Greek artists, at a time when Rome had just been abandoned and was entering on a period of difficulty and austerity.

The character of the newly instituted cults is no less signi' ficant. The triads of Jupiter, Juno and Minerva on the one hand and Ceres, Liber and Libera on the other have a Tyrrhenian appearance, while the god Saturn was of Italic origin. The cult of the Dioscuri came from the Etrusco'Latin town of Tuscu' lum. Lastly the temples of the agrarian divinities and of Mercury, situated close to each other, were patronized by the plebs, who looked to these gods for protection and guidance. In fact, the sanctuary of Ceres, Liber and Libera on the Aventine became the religious centre of the plebeian commu' nity. All these important facts become explicable, it seems to me, if the Etruscan leaders had not yet left Rome and were continuing to support the plebs against the landed proprietors of Latin stock. The latter reacted violently as soon as the Etruscans left, in about 475. This view also renders explicable a curious aspect of classical Rome: of the consuls at the begin' ning of the Republic, a certain number, among whom were Spurius Cassius and Junius Brutus, came from plebeian families. If at the beginning of the consular magistrature the Etruscans were still present, as I believe, they could have allowed the plebs to elect some of their most outstanding representatives into office.

In fact, Rome's history during the first quarter of the fifth century seems in every way similar to that of Latium as a whole and Etruria. Here again archaeology provides us with reliable data. Despite the inadequacy of the excavations undertaken in many Latin towns and the fact that some of them were carried out some time ago we possess, for this period, important frag/ Plates 48, 49, 52 ments of cult/statues, many architectonic terracottas from Lanu/ vium, Satricum near Antium, and Civita Castellana. Thus the Latin and Faliscan towns also went through a period of great activity in religious building at the beginning of the fifth century, just as Rome did; as at Rome, the character of the decoration of the Latin sanctuaries is typically Etruscan, or sometimes, as at Satricum, Etrusco/Greek. It is hard to imagine that this architectural and religious boom, which stopped soon after in both the Latin cities and Rome, could have followed the Etruscans' departure. It is much more likely to have preceded it.

The conclusion suggested by all this seems clear. The evolu/ tion of a political system, in the sense of the Republic, at Rome must have begun towards the end of the sixth century; and, as aforesaid, the change from a royalty of a sacred character to a régime in which power was exercised, collegially or not, by magistrates nominated for varying periods was a phenomenon common to numerous Latin, Etruscan and Osco/Umbrian cities, and by no means peculiar to Rome. Here and there the *rex* was replaced by a simple, supreme magistrate or a pair of magistrates in the form of praetors or consuls. There is therefore no reason to doubt that such a transformation did in fact take place in Rome at the end of the sixth century; the consuls had, moreover, a power which Livy calls the *regium imperium*. On the other hand, the final departure of the Etruscans did not take place until about thirty years later. Thus the Ancients, and after them the Moderns, fused together two separate sequences of events which, as I have tried to show elsewhere,[1] took place at different times: the beginnings of a régime with republican tendencies on the one hand and the departure of the Etruscan tyrants on the other. This throws a new light on a crucial period for Rome which the classical historians, unable to understand close or distant relationships between cities and regions of ancient Italy, wrongly simplified.

I myself believe that I have found an explanation[2] in the only sure basis of the chronology, in the date of the dedication of the Temple of Jupiter Capitolinus, namely, 13 September 509. For the Capitoline temple, which was to become the very symbol of Rome and the Empire, could not remain, in the eyes of the Romans, a purely Etruscan work, since the Etruscans had from the fifth century B.C. become the mortal enemies of the *Urbs*. The strict Roman conscience demanded that at least the dedication of the temple should be Roman.

The annals also make the Etruscans disappear, as if by a miracle, a few months before this dedication which purports to mark a return to the authentic Roman.

CULTURE IN TARQUINIAN ROME

The Tarquins were a typical Etruscan monarchy; as heads of state they were also chief justices, army leaders and high priests. Their absolute power was embodied in a series of outward attributes which remained traditional in Rome, but were transferred to the chief magistrate and the *triumphator*, who wore a gold crown, gold ring and sceptre. Their state apparel was the *toga palmata*; the lictors who accompanied them bore *fasces* on their shoulders, as a sign of omnipotence. According to Silius Italicus (*Punica*, VIII, 484), these were first introduced by

---

[1] 'Rome de 509 à 475 environ avant J. C.' *Revue des Etudes latines,* Vol. XXXVII, 1960.

[2] Set forth in an article in *Revue de l'Histoire des Religions*, 1961.

Vetulonia. At the end of the last century, excavations in a cemetery in Vetulonia revealed remains of a *fasces* from which emerged a bipennate axe: the whole is made of iron and, like the tomb where it was discovered (now called the Tomb of the Lictor), dates from the seventh century B.C. Here again archaeology confirms the authenticity of the literary tradition. This material sign of the sovereign's power—the rods for flogging and the axe as a symbol of supreme authority—con, tinued in Rome after the departure of the Etruscans and the beginning of the Republican régime. It was then transferred to the consuls, who wielded supreme authority over the legions, though only for one year. In the same way, the triumphal ceremonies celebrated after Republican Rome's victories perpetuated the religious rites carried out by the Etruscan kings after the downfall of their enemies. During this solemn proces, sion, which ended with a sacrifice to Jupiter on the Capitol, the king, standing on his war chariot and heading the long line of soldiers and prisoners, was temporarily identified with the war-god himself.

The succession of Etruscan kings was certainly not a purely Roman affair as described by the traditional story, and the ambitions of foreign towns and chieftains must have weighed heavily at the moment of succession to the Roman throne. The remarkable Etruscan frescoes on the François tomb at Vulci demonstrate this and give the Etruscan version of the events which led to Servius Tullius's accession. The Emperor Claudius, an experienced Etruscologist, says in effect in his famous speech, preserved on the bronze tablet of Lyon, that in Etruscan Servius Tullius's name was Mastarna. One of the scenes decorating the François Tomb represents an episode involving Mastarna fighting one of the Tarquins. The François Tomb is a truly monumental structure; its entrance corridor seems to take the visitor into the bowels of the earth. Originally an impressive collection of paintings decorated certain of its rooms, but as they were damaged and in danger of further dilapidation, they were skilfully removed from the walls in 1862 and are now in the Torlonia Museum, Rome. According to experts, their dates range between the fourth and second centuries B.C. The tomb belonged to a rich Vulcian family, by the name of Satie.

Several of the sections show mythological scenes, such as the sacrifice of Trojan prisoners offered up by Achilles to the Manes of Patroclus. But for our purposes the most interesting are the scenes illustrating the ancient history of Vulci. A series of warriors, either naked or wearing arms and cloaks, are arranged in pairs. There is a picture of one, Caile Vipinas, being freed by a man called Macstrna. Then there are four pairs of fighters. The losers are identified by their names followed by the names of their native city. Among them is Cneve Tarchunies Rumach, i.e. Gnaeus Tarquin of Rome. One of the conquerors is called Avle Vipinas. There was thus a battle between Avle Vipinas, Caile Vipinas and Macstrna on the one hand and Cneve Tarchunies Rumach on the other, in which the last-named was defeated. Now, the Etruscan names refer to the characters frequently mentioned by Roman writers as forming part of Rome's primitive history. Macstrna was definitely the Mastarna mentioned by Claudius, i.e. Servius Tullius, who reigned between the two Tarquins. Tarchunies Rumach is Tarquin of Rome, the king whom Mastarna succeeded, not by being nominated by the Romans but by means of a military victory over his predecessor. Avle and Caile Vipinas are known to us under the romanized name of the Vibenna brothers and they also took part in the drama of monarchic Rome. Here, then, is the graphic presentation of the succession of Servius Tullius to Tarquin the Elder in its Etruscan version, in which Servius Mastarna is a *condottiere* from Vulci who with the help of fellow-townsmen fights and dethrones the king of Rome.

Plate 54

This version is of considerable interest in many ways. First, in this fresco Etruscan art takes on a historical aspect. This tendency seems, in fact, to be characteristic of many Italic peoples. A similar trait can be seen both in Republican and Imperial Rome, where art was of documentary and narrative inspiration. For the Roman artist the history of the city itself was to fulfil the same function as mythological fables and stories of heroes and gods had done for the Greeks. In reality, it is the historical bas-reliefs, such as the celebrated frieze on Trajan's Column, which best illustrate the specific Roman genius. The Vulcian painter who decorated the François Tomb some sixty miles north of Rome heralded the beginning of a movement that was to sweep over the whole of the peninsula.

Secondly—and this is of particular importance to us in our attempt to analyse the traditional Roman account—these frescoes show clearly how much historico-legendary traditions dealing with the distant past varied from town to town. The chronicles, oral at first, then written and finally immortalized in artistic representations, naturally exalted the exploits of the local warriors and chiefs. Consequently the same episodes took on a very different appearance in the different places where they were remembered. In the present instance the Vulcian and Roman traditions differ widely and it is now impossible to reconstruct the true story with any exactitude. However, since the subject is Rome, the Roman version is naturally more suspect of alterations, made to satisfy national pride. The *condottieri* of Vulci, who appear in the fresco with Mastarna, really existed and fought at the end of the sixth century B.C. At Veii a fragment of a *bucchero* vase from this period was found, bearing an inscription containing the name Avile Vipiennas, i.e. Aulus Vibenna.[1] Thus the throne of Rome was the stake for which various army leaders from different towns fought, and the expeditions of the Vibenna brothers, Mastarna

[1] *Studi Etruschi*, XIII, 1939, p. 455.

and subsequently Porsenna, resulted in the installation in Rome of powerful overlords who already ruled over Vulci and Clusium respectively. These raids stemmed partly, of course, from the ambition of the generals concerned; but they also show the interest in Rome, as a key position, taken by the powerful lucumonies of western and central Etruria. Vulci and Clusium reached the zenith of their power at the end of the sixth and beginning of the fifth century. In each case the town's relationship with Campania played a large part in the progress of its power and wealth. From Vulci the route to Campania led along the seacoast; from Clusium it was accessible through the valley of the Tiber. It was because Rome dominated both these routes that it was so greatly prized as a site. Consequently, by reason both of the *condottieri*'s ambitions and pressing strategic needs, the throne of the Tarquins became the object of lively competition, if not desperate battles. All of which is far removed from the purely internal quarrels of the Roman annalists' patriotic accounts.

The monarchic institutions in Rome were paralleled at the same time in many other Latin and Etruscan cities. But it is necessary, as has been stressed before, to cast our nets even wider and consider also what was happening in southern Italy and Sicily at about 500 B.C. This was a time of tyrannical rulers who increased the power of their cities and their cultural expansion and who drew their support from new social classes, in opposition to the old oligarchies. A similar process was occurring in Agrigentum, Syracuse and Cumae. Events in Etruria, Latium and Rome itself, indeed, bear a strong resemblance to this very marked political phenomenon in Magna Graecia and Sicily. It was, in fact, a historical process in which a large part of Italy was concerned and which introduced the cultural *Koiné* which has already been mentioned. The centre of Italy was profoundly influenced by the Greek cities of the south, particularly Cumae, and there is no reason to limit this influence to art and religion: it extended also to the political and social spheres.

As far as the foreign policy of the Tarquins is concerned, we are reduced to hypotheses. But it is very likely that under their government Rome exercised a form of hegemony over the surrounding Latin cities. This would correspond with the victorious wars which the Etruscan kings waged, according to tradition, against the Sabines and the peoples of Latium. The foundation on the Aventine of a federal sanctuary dedicated to Diana is a concrete sign of the political and religious supremacy of the city. The new temple replaced the old sanctuary of Aricia, the one/time centre of the Alban league, and this urge for substitution is also shown in the choice of the date for the foundation, August 13, the date of the Feast of Aricia. The Aventine Diana, protector of women and slaves, standing in the middle of an important market, was to be one of the favourite divinities of the Roman plebs.

The internal structure, both political and social, of Tarquin/ ian Rome raised difficult problems on which opinion is very divided. It is impossible to tackle them without first considering the analogies offered by the contemporary Italic and Greek communities. The opposition between different social groups, which was to become so marked under the Republic, can be seen to a greater or lesser degree all over Italy. The archaic monarchs had relied on an oligarchy of landed proprietors who fought on horseback or in chariots. But now, with the develop/ ment of cities and of trade on land and sea, new classes emerged who swelled the ranks of those who fought on foot. As well as the patricians, who were grouped in *gentes*—large families, all of whose members could claim a common ancestor, and who had the monopoly of public honours and priest/ hoods—there gradually grew up the *populus*, which had a long struggle before it attained equal rights. But it had already been introduced into the city by the Etruscan kings; this is the reality behind the so-called Servian reforms which replaced the division into *curiae* by the centuriate system. The traditional story, which retained the memory of this basic change, ante- dated later reforms, whereby the rights and duties of every Roman citizen came to be determined by his financial resources which were fixed by the census.

In the sphere of art, excavations of archaic Rome have amply Plates 43-7, 50, 51 demonstrated the high creative level reached in the Etruscan period. The architectonic terracottas are comparable with those *Figs. 16, 17* found in large numbers at Veii and Cerveteri. In Rome, as in these towns, the figures decorating the temples must have made up a magnificent gallery of portraits of heroes and gods. In the period we are dealing with, productions in Latium differed from those in Etruria only in betraying a trace of provincialism and, often, a pleasant simplicity in the treatment of groups and facial expressions. But this trait is more pro- nounced in centres like Lanuvium than at Rome. Plate 52

In art, Rome came very close to Etruria, and this fact is often indicated by tradition. Certain features of the traditional account concern important and general aspects of Etruscan art as a whole and not only purely Roman art. It is well known that Greek influence had a profound effect on Tuscan artists at different stages of their history. Some scholars, struck by this constant interaction, have concluded that Tuscan art was entirely un- original, that it was merely a provincial reflection of Greek art. Such a conclusion is forced and certainly incorrect. Etruscan works are not mere servile copies of Greek ones, and one need only go from a Greek room in a museum to an Etruscan room to be fully aware of this. Greece was a source of inspiration, but it did not stifle all the originality of Etruria's quite different character.

Etruria constantly imported Greek productions of every kind, and one has to refer back to these models to appreciate Etruscan reactions towards them. In Rome itself, it must be remembered, large quantities of Attic vases, at first with black-figure and later with red-figure decoration, were imported during the Etruscan period. Textual evidence adds further details which point to the presence of Greek immigrants in Etruria and links this presence with either the royal family itself, or the decoration of one sacred building or another.

According to Pliny the Elder (XXXV, 152 and 154), Demaratus, the father of Tarquin the Elder, came to Etruria from Corinth, accompanied by *koroplathoi* bearing the honourable names of Eucheir, Diopos and Eugrammos. These were the three artists who were reputed to have taught Italy the art of sculpture in terracotta, at which they excelled. We cannot, of course, say exactly how much truth lies behind this legend. But it certainly reflects the profound influence exercised by the Peloponnesian art of Corinth on Etruscan art as a whole from the seventh century B.C. There is even a curious agreement between Pliny's dates and those attested by archaeology. According to the traditional story, Tarquin the Elder ascended the throne in 616, which placed the arrival in Italy of his father and the Corinthian artists accompanying him roughly in the middle of the seventh century B.C. Now, this is exactly the time when the small perfume-vases called proto-Corinthian began to appear on Etruscan territory and at Rome itself; these indicate commercial relations with Corinth on the one hand and Etruria and Latium on the other. After this, Corinthian vases continued to be imported for a considerable time, and large quantities of the derivative pottery known as Italo-Corinthian or Etrusco-Corinthian were made on the spot. It can be seen from this that the legend, when it told of the arrival of Corinthian artists before the beginning of the Tarquinian dynasty, was embodying a real and profound artistic influence from which Rome, like Latium and Etruria, benefited.

There were, in fact, Greeks actually living in various parts of Etruria in small colonies of merchants during the archaic

Plate 40
Fig. 14

period; their presence is attested epigraphically from a very early date in Caere and later in Spina, the Etruscan city at the mouth of the Po. Objects have been found in Etruria which could only have come from a Greek workshop; these are the famous *hydriai* with black-figure decoration, made in Cerveteri by a Greek from Asiatic Ionia who probably came to Tuscany at about the middle of the sixth century B.C. With regard to Rome, we have exact information given us by Pliny and Elder himself. A temple, dedicated in 493 B.C., and so in any case in a Rome still under Etruscan influence, was decorated by two Greek artists. The temple was, in fact, a sanctuary dedicated to three fertility divinities, Ceres the ancient goddess of growing things, and Liber and Libera who presided over animal reproduction. A recent thesis[1] analyses in detail the origin of such a grouping and the character of the new temple, which was to become particularly popular with the plebeians. Two Greek artists, named by Pliny, carried out the decoration in the following way: 'The most famous modellers were Damophilos and Gorgasos, who were also painters. They ornamented the temple of Ceres in Rome, near the *Circus Maximus*, with their works in the two different arts and they indicated by an inscription in Greek verse that the work on the right was by Damophilos and that on the left by Gorgasos.' (Pliny the Elder, XXXV, 154) It was quite natural for Etruria and Latium to have such plastic and pictorial decoration done by Greeks; their artistic culture was at that time deeply influenced by Greece. Does this indicate the Hellenization at this early date of agrarian cults of typically Latin origin and character? I would hesitate to draw this conclusion. It is enough to say that decoration of this kind, so in tune with the taste of the period, might well have facilitated the later Hellenization of both gods and religion.

Thus, many aspects of Etruscan Rome are reminiscent of

[1] See Bibliography, p. 160 (Le Bonniec, H.).

other large Tuscan cities. Archaeology brings clear confirma⁄
tion of this. It would be even clearer if during the course of
Rome's long history the constant building and rebuilding on
the same sites had not inevitably destroyed the most archaic
levels. The loss of some of the more valuable material, however,
has been repaired to a certain extent by patient research, so that
the most distant periods of Rome's history can now be seen
with tolerable clarity. Small settlements, no doubt of various
origins, were welded organically into a town. For two centuries
its culture grew, progressively though slowly, thanks to impor⁄
tations and influences from many quarters though principally
from Magna Graecia. The installation of the Etruscans on the
banks of the Tiber brought the small kingdom within the
Tyrrhenian orbit; the classical account ignores this fact,
although it persisted in popular memory in the form of the
story of a simple change of dynasties and the substitution of
foreigners from the rich north for the Latin kings. But the
legacy left by the Etruscans was still an ever⁄present reality to
the Romans of the classical period. We have already referred
briefly to various cultural influences exercised by the Tyr⁄
rhenians, but now we must go more deeply into the complex
questions of Roman language and religion. It is difficult to
draw any hard⁄and⁄fast conclusions. If the Etruscans taught
the ancient Romans a great deal of practical knowledge and
bequeathed to them many features of daily life and outward
manifestations of political power, they had no comparable
influence on the language of Rome, its modes of thought or
ways of envisaging the connexions between the sacred and the
secular world. In these all⁄important domains the Latins on the
banks of the Tiber clung tenaciously to their own traditions;
when the Tyrrhenian invaders returned to the region from
which they had been impelled to depart by a powerful urge to
expand, neither the Roman language nor the Roman religion
were greatly different from what they had been a century earlier.

CHAPTER VI

The Language, Law and Religion
of Primitive Rome

THE LATIN LANGUAGE, shared by all the villages—later to become towns—of Latium, owed the supreme position which it has now occupied for nearly three thousand years to the fortunes of Rome. At the beginning, however, the area where Latin was spoken was very small and completely surrounded by huge regions occupied by languages that might have seemed, at the time, much more likely to prevail. History decided otherwise.

Earlier, we pointed out the extreme complexity of the linguistic situation in an Italy occupied from the Early Iron Age by peoples of different origins and with different cultures. The position of Latin within this great dialectal variety poses many serious problems to the linguists, who have not yet seen their way to solving them completely.

Fig. 3

Convincing analogies have been discovered between the common ancestor, Indo-European, and the languages attested during the historical period, and these have led to the hypothesis of intermediate linguistic unities; in the regions with which we are concerned, these would have been Italo-Celtic and Italic unities preceding the multitude of dialects scattered over the peninsula. This theory is strongly attacked by linguists who deny the existence of such intermediate unities at any time during the prehistoric or protohistoric periods. According to them, Osco-Umbrian and Latin are independent languages with characters so different that they could never at any time have been one and the same tongue. They merely belong to the same zone within the area served by Indo-European; but they had no common ancestor peculiar to themselves. The question is a complex one which depends on numerous non-linguistic arguments, in particular archaeological ones, for support. But it is extremely difficult to arrive at a synthesis between archae/ology and linguistics, particularly when dealing with remote periods for which the material evidence gained from excava/tions is scanty and capable of varying interpretations. Conse/quently the question remains open and the nature of the verdict depends upon the importance attached by the inquirer to the structural similarities between Osco/Umbrian and Latin. The clash of different opinions has, however, proved fruitful, as so often happens, and has clarified our ideas about the over/all linguistic picture in primitive Italy.

Among the Italic languages the nearest to Latin are Venetic, spoken in the region of the Po estuary, Faliscan, a dialectal variation of Latin from the lower valley of the Tiber, and probably Siculan. All have an archaic character which would be explained if they had been introduced by an early wave of invaders preceding the Osco/Umbrians. According to this hypothesis, a migration of 'proto/Latins' swept over the peninsula from north to south, leaving ethnic and linguistic signposts here and there. At the end of the journey the various groups were isolated from each other. If the Latins preserved their particular archaic dialect in all its semantic purity, this was mainly due to their early organization and innate tendencies towards conservatism.

'Latin' is usually thought of as being the language of Rome. This is quite understandable; when writing developed, Rome already occupied a privileged position in Latium, and the other Latin towns soon ceased to use their local dialects which were rapidly being supplanted by the Latin of Rome. In primitive Latium, however, there were various languages dif/ferentiated by dialectal variations, as can be seen from a number of surviving inscriptions. The only two towns whose languages are tolerably well known to us are Falerii, north of the Tiber, the centre of the Faliscan region which was from the begin/ning profoundly influenced by Etruria, and Praeneste, about twenty-five miles east of Rome. We know Faliscan from a number of important texts; it appears to have been a Latin dialect which was modified by both Sabine and Etruscan influences. In the light of recent archaeological discoveries and the progress made in the study of its dialect, it would appear that the region round Falerii deserves a historical account to itself; we have already remarked on the importance of its commercial relations with Rome in the first two centuries. But it is the language of Praeneste which gives the clearest picture of the language of a Latin town other than Rome. Even here Roman Latin exercised an early influence and inscriptions show only traces of the local language. However, the oldest surviving Latin inscription is engraved on a fine golden fibula which was discovered in a Praenestean tomb, probably the rich Etruscan tomb which has been given the name of Bernardini. The fibula is now in the Pigorini Prehistoric Museum in Rome; it dates from about 600 B.C. The short text on it is, therefore, earlier by at least a century than the earliest Latin inscription found on the site of Rome, the *Lapis Niger*, which we shall deal with later. It reads: *Manios med fhefhaked Numasioi*, which in classical Latin would be: *Manius me fecit Numerio*, meaning 'Manius made me for Numerius'. Certain peculiarities of the language can be accounted for by the very early date of the inscription, but the reduplication of the verb is typically Praenestean.

Dialectal variations of this kind, which gradually yielded to the prestige of Roman Latin, left few written traces. They nevertheless had a lasting influence on Roman Latin itself, and even gave it a certain number of typically rural word-forms. As A. Meillet says: 'The Latin which finally crystallized was the language not of a cultured urban class but of an aristocracy of skilled peasants able to draw on a wide cultural area by which they were influenced.'[1]

[1] See Bibliography, p. 158 (*Esquisse d'une histoire de la langue latine*).

For some time scholars have been devoting detailed study to Latin's borrowings at different dates—though from a very early period—from the Aegean, Greek and Etruscan languages. The Indo-European peoples knew nothing of certain crops and plants which were, on the other hand, familiar to the peoples of the Mediterranean. From the latter the tribes newly arrived in southern Europe, and Italy in particular, borrowed the names of plants and other objects of which they had hitherto been ignorant. Often, parallel words were borrowed in both Latin and Greek; this was the case with the Hellenic and Latin words for wine, rose, lily, cypress and fig. In certain cases Etruscan acted as an intermediary, introducing words into the Latin languages.

As might be expected, Latin borrowings from Greek were both early and important. From a very early date, as morpho-logical analysis shows, elements of the Greek vocabulary passed into use at Rome. These were mainly cultural terms describing customs, techniques and objects which the Latins—at the beginning of their history, as later—received from the superior culture developed by the Greeks first in Greece, subsequently in southern Italy. There was, for example, the word *machina*, borrowed from the Dorian μαχανά, which meant an ingenious method of obtaining a result, a machine. In the same way *machina* in Latin meant 'invention' and, in the concrete sense, 'machine', 'device'. Different technical usages gave it the specialized senses of 'engine of war', 'scaffolding', or 'machine for lifting weights'. Similarly a word as important as *poena*, meaning 'compensation for a fault or crime', 'ransom', 'fine', 'punishment', 'chastisement', is a direct borrowing from the Dorian ποινά. Like most Greek loan-words, *poena* was prob-ably at the beginning a popular expression denoting the punish-ment inflicted on a servant. Of names of objects, *oliva* and *oleum* were borrowed at an early date from the Greek tongues of southern Italy.

Etruscan also left many tràces in the Roman language. In fact, discoveries have shown that in Tarquinian Rome Etruscan was spoken concurrently with Latin. Two recently found *bucchero* vases, one from the slopes of the Capitol, the other from the top of the Palatine, bear Etruscan inscriptions which are contemporary with the earliest Latin epigraphical texts, and thus prove the bilingualism of the city in the sixth century B.C. But it was at an even earlier date that Latin received its most valuable legacy from the Etruscans—their alphabet. The prob/ lem of the origin of the Latin alphabet, which evoked consider/ able argument over a long period, is now solved. It was not, as was often suggested, taken from the Greeks of Cumae, but from the Latins' northern neighbours, the Etruscans. This is sufficiently proved by the order of the voiced and unvoiced gutterals, C and G, in the Latin alphabet. This order, different from that in Greek, is due to the absence of voiced consonants in Etruscan which, when it adopted the Greek alphabet, interpreted *gamma* as a voiceless consonant. The Latins gave the third letter both values, then, to obviate all ambiguity, introduced a new seventh letter into their alphabet, G, which took over the duties of the Greek *gamma*.

Plate 53

Loan/alphabets were far from being a peculiarly Latin phenomenon. Apart from Messapian, all the Indo/European languages of Italy, Faliscan, Venetic, Oscan, Umbrian and Lepontic, used alphabets derived from the Etruscan alphabet. In no case, of course, was the derived alphabet a copy, pure and simple, of the Etruscan; each was an original adaptation, and all were made at different times. By means of various elements it is possible to give an approximate date to the adaptations; these, of course, preceded the earliest inscriptions in each local script. But these very ancient texts are often difficult to date in themselves; and it is in any case possible that earlier inscriptions have been lost. At all events the Latin alphabet was borrowed from the Etruscans and adapted to

Latin needs during the seventh century: it could not have been earlier, because Etruscan culture only started to develop in about 700 B.C.; it could not have been later, because the Praenestean fibula must date from before 600 B.C.

The Latin vocabulary contains a certain number of words of Etruscan origin. Sometimes their derivation is alluded to by the Ancients themselves, as in the case of *histrio*=actor, *subulo* =flute-player, and *atrium*, the name of a room in the Roman house. Sometimes it is deduced by modern linguists. A typical case is the important word *persona*. This originally meant the mask of an actor, but then came to mean in turn the role attributed to the mask, the characteristics of the role, the character himself, and finally a person. In this last sense it passed into the vocabularies of all the Romance languages except Rumanian. The ending in *-na* is in itself an indication of possible Etruscan origin, in default of any other etymology. But, in addition, curious masked characters appear on several frescoes discovered at Tarquinia which date from the end of the sixth century B.C.; the word *phersu* is written by the side

Plate 57

of one of them. They are in the Tomb of the Augurs and the so-called *tomba del pulcinella*, both discovered at an early date but only recently subjected to exhaustive examination. In 1958 research methods based on the electrical resistivity of the soil disclosed a new and very interesting painted tomb representing alongside athletic scenes and very lively chariot races a new *phersu*. This new find has been described in a book recently published in Italy.[1] All these *phersu* are masked dancers taking part in races or cruel sports which might be the proto-types of the Roman gladiatorial games. Their name is signi-ficant; *phersu* means the mask and the masked character, and it is certain that the Latin word derived from the Etruscan. This loan-word is of the same order as *subulo* and *histrio*. The Etruscans were fond of singing, music and sports. Flute-players

[1] See Bibliography, p. 159 (Bartoccini, R., Lerici, C. M., Moretti, M.).

and mimetic dancers occupied a special place in their religious and private life. The Roman historians knew that on certain occasions Rome had summoned jugglers and mimes, as for instance in 364 B.C. when, to ward off the terrible scourge of the plague, scenic games were organized in which actors specially summoned from Etruria participated (Livy, VII, 2, 4). But long before this the terms denoting these different sorts of actors and musicians had passed from Etruscan into Latin, and among them was the word *persona* which was to have such a brilliant future. Note that the semantic develop‑ ment of the Greek πρόσωπον was parallel with that of *persona*, but the link between the Greek and Etruscan words is difficult to clarify.

These examples show how ready Latin was to absorb both Etruscan and Greek. It should not be forgotten, either, that a good number of Roman proper names were also of Etruscan origin. Nevertheless, despite all this, the language was not radically modified and the basic Latin vocabulary remained. It includes relatively few terms that cannot be traced to Indo‑ European. The Etruscan invasion modified certain characteris‑ tics of Roman culture, but it did not undermine the solid structure of its archaic language, based as it was on a firm rural foundation.

It would be useful to be able to study the Latin of the first centuries more closely. But the number of known inscriptions dating from before the third century B.C. is extremely limited, half a dozen at the most; whilst for the earlier periods, the beginning of the fifth century, for instance, there are no epigra‑ phical texts other than those on the fibula of Praeneste, the *Lapis Niger*, the new inscription of Lavinium and the so‑called *Duenos* vase. The first, though very clear, is also short; the other three raise serious problems of interpretation. But this is hardly surprising. Inevitably Latin underwent great changes between its origins and the classical period, and by the latter time even

Fig. 21

the Romans could not understand the most archaic texts. According to Quintilian (*Institutions*, I, 6, 40), the Salian priests of his time sang a hymn in such an ancient language that the Ancients themselves had difficulty in understanding the words.

However, the oldest of the Roman inscriptions, that on the *Lapis Niger*, which had resisted numerous attempts to decipher it, has just been partially interpreted by means of an ingenious comparison with a text from the classical period. Several ancient authors speak of a place on the Roman Forum which bore the name of *Lapis Niger*, the Black Stone. They all agree that this was a burial site occupied, according to some, by the father of King Tullus Hostilius, according to others, by Faustulus, Romulus's foster-father, who fell there while fighting against the Sabines, and, according to the third party, by Plate 21   Romulus himself. Now, in 1898, a very ancient monument was discovered on the Forum where the *Comitium*, *Rostra*, *Curia* and Arch of Septimus Severus meet. It is composed of a square platform made up of six strips of black marble. A sort of railing of narrow slabs of white marble about three feet high and set up on end acted as a barrier and marked the boundary of the area. And beneath the black marble paving were found ancient and enigmatic structures and the base of a rectangular cippus made of tufa with ancient inscriptions on its various surfaces.

It is difficult to give an exact date to this *boustrophedon* inscription. Nevertheless its paleographic characteristics suggest that it can be assigned to about 500 B.C. or the end of the monarchic period. Parts of it have disappeared owing to the crumbling of the stone; but the remaining text, however incomplete and obscure, has given rise to numerous widely different interpretations. Only the beginning is clearly comprehensible: *Quoiho* ... *sakros . esed*, is the equivalent of the classical Latin *qui hu*[*nc lapidem*] (or *hu*[*ic lapidi*] . . .) *sacer erit*, meaning: 'He who (damages) this (stone) will be cursed.' This was the archaic formula for the supreme curse to be laid on anyone imprudent or impious enough to lay hands on a sacred monument.

In the very fragmentary lines that follow—and there is nothing to indicate the importance of the missing portions—there are several words which can be deciphered with certainty: *recei, kalatorem, iouxmenta, kapia(d)*. Now these words, and others that are more enigmatic, can be explained by reference to a rule of the art of augury mentioned by Cicero, who was himself an augur, in his treatise *De Divinatione* (II, 36). He writes: '*Huic simile est, quod nos augures praecipimus, ne juge(s) auspicium obveniat, ut jumenta jubeant dijungere.*' This may be translated as: 'In the same way, to prevent the unfortunate appearance of a *juge(s) auspicium*, we augurs prescribe that they order the beasts of burden to be unyoked.' This passage refers to the precautions that the priests and magistrates were to take to prevent un-favourable auspices from interrupting enterprises that had already begun. So, to avoid the danger of the *juge(s) auspicium* which was produced if a passing yoked team (=*junctum jumen-tum*) dropped its excrements, the augurs ordered their servants, the *kalatores*, to unyoke the beasts of burden. The Romans' practical cast of mind enabled them to hold all the trumps in the complicated god-man game. They made sure that the augurs, passing along the *Via Sacra* in the opposite direction from the Capitol, could draw attention to a possible *juge(s) auspicium* as they reached the first cross-street, the *Vicus Jugarius*, the part of the Forum nearest to the *Lapis Niger*. We know from Cicero's *De Divinatione*, I, 40, that augural divination was one of the privileges of the king of Rome; and in fact the word *rex* in its archaic dative form *recei* (*regi*) appears in this inscrip-tion. It was here that he had inscribed on a stone protected by religious taboos the text of the sacred law destined to facilitate one of his chief priestly duties.

Latin epigraphical texts, which are so scanty for the

Fig. 19 Etrusco-Roman mirror from Praeneste, now in the British Museum. It probably dates from the third century B.C. and shows a scene from daily life, a young man and woman playing a game which resembles backgammon. Above them are Latin inscriptions whose meaning has been a subject of controversy. The girl is saying 'devincam ted'—'I shall beat you', and the man is replying 'opeinor'—'yes, I think you will'. The last letter of 'opeinor' is an 'r' engraved in the Etruscan manner, the language of Praeneste having been strongly influenced by Etruscan. cf. E. Gerhard, Die Etruskischen Spiegel, V, p. 146.

monarchic period and the first two centuries of the Republic, become more numerous in the third century B.C. Some of these inscriptions, though not within the time-scheme laid down for this book, are of help in solving interesting problems concern, ing the most remote periods in Latium. This was the case recently with the vexed question of the exact siting of an ancient sanctuary surrounded by a sacred wood, the *Lucus Feroniae*, in the Capena region. Here there was a strong cult of Feronia (a divinity who had originated in the Sabine mountains) which is attested from the 'kingship' period. From the seventh century the *Lucus* was a sacred spot and asylum, as well as a thriving trading centre. It was the attacks on the grove's inviolability which, according to tradition, gave rise to the war between Tullus Hostilius and the Sabines. The Roman king com, plained that Roman merchants were arrested in the temple of Feronia at the height of the trading; the Sabines complained that certain of their merchants who had taken refuge in the sacred grove had been taken prisoner by Rome (Livy, I, 30, 5). This passage gives us a good idea of the complex character of the oldest sanctuaries in Latium. From the beginning their religious and commercial sides were closely linked, so that they were often used for important fairs and markets.

Much later, during the second Punic War, the Capena Sanctuary was sacked by the Carthaginians. In 211, according to Livy, Hannibal entered the Capena region and delivered the *Lucus*, which was famed for its wealth, into the impious hands of his soldiers (Livy, XXVI, 11). Until quite recently no traces of the famous temple had been found. But the dis, covery in 1952 of archaic inscriptions dedicated to Feronia inside an important *favissa* containing a large number of pottery votive offerings put an end to doubt. The votive objects evidently belonged to the sanctuary, which must therefore have been situated near the junction of the Capenas, a small tributary of the Tiber, and the Tiber itself, at the place known as Scorano. A few traces of Carthaginian vandalism were still visible: several small stone bases to which bronze statuettes were originally attached were found without them, the statuettes having been removed by the enemy, who collected so much loot that according to the Ancients they had to leave heaps of bronze behind them.

Certain features of the dedications to Feronia—the name of one of the dedicators and the use of a word probably of Sabine origin to describe the sanctuary—lead one to think of the Sabine region from which the goddess originally came.

The oldest Latin texts are thus interesting on many levels, and a study of them is useful for a knowledge of the history of primitive Rome. If they are still difficult to date, this gap may be filled in by closer co-operation between the archaeologist and the epigraphist. Already objects bearing inscriptions can often be adequately dated according to their type or character. Here, as in many other fields, it is clear that collaboration between specialists of different kinds is an absolute necessity.

Fig. 19

THE RELIGION OF ROME
IN THE FIRST CENTURIES

The study of the origins of Rome takes us back to the sources of the Roman religion and the beginning of a religious history that was to last over a thousand years and to present a curious mixture of two apparently irreconcilable characteristics, a deeply ingrained conservatism and a constant readiness to absorb strange religions, one after another, into the native cult. Thanks to the results yielded by research, it is now possible to distinguish more clearly between the periods of this long history and to identify the many elements which went to make up this exceptionally involved cult-complex.

One must not be deceived by the apparent frigidity and methodical quality of the Roman religion in the classical period. Taboos and practices of magical inspiration crop up again and again in Roman life. And the 'sacred' had an importance similar to that revealed by comparative research in widely differing societies. Throughout the world, religion pre╱ supposes an opposition between natural life and a domain ruled by fear and hope. By definition, a religious man is one who acknowledges these two complementary spheres. The opposition between them is a fundamental human idea, the realization of the sacred, a kind of sensibility. The sacred object is under an interdict. Contact with it is dangerous. But it is ambivalent, alternately benevolent and malevolent, and it is also the source of all effective action. Man must rigorously separate the sacred from the profane. In fact, the essential function of religious rites is to regulate the links between the profane and the sacred: consecration rites introduce profane objects into the sacred sphere; deconsecration rites restore sacred objects to the profane world; prohibition rites or taboos estab╱ lish strict barriers between the two worlds; finally, the function of expiation rites is to wipe out contamination.

This dialectical approach is manifest in Roman thought, rites and vocabulary. Let us start with the definition[1] of the word *sacer*:

Things which are *sacra* are opposed to things which are *profana*. That which is *sacrum* belongs to the world of the gods and differs essentially from that which belongs to the daily life of men. The leap from the *sacer* to the *profanus* is accomplished by means of definite rites, and the two categories are clearly defined. The idea *sacer* is not identical with either *good* or *bad*; it is altogether separate. A thing which is *sacer* cannot be touched without being contaminated or con╱ taminating. Hence the double meaning of *sacred* and *cursed*. The guilty man sacrificed to the gods is also *sacer* (*sacer esto*).

[1] From *Dictionnaire étymologique de la langue latine* by Ernout, A., and Meillet, A. (see Bibliography, p. 158).

Curiously enough, the formula for the handing-over of the committer of sacrilege to divine justice appears, as we have seen, in the text of the oldest Roman inscription. But is this, in fact, surprising? Sacred formulae of magical origin are always most important to a culture at the beginning of its history. It is one of the achievements of modern jurists to have recognized and stated the close connexion, at the time of the origin of peoples and towns, between religion and law, the latter being shaped and moulded by religious and magical elements. This applies to the most ancient rules of Roman law known to us from the classical authors; the jurists of the Imperial period held them to be *leges regiae,* laws adopted by the *comitia curiata* at an early date, after having been proposed by one or other of the Roman kings. But it has been shown that these were not real laws, but only very ancient rules the authority for which came from the sphere of primitive magic. Such was the case with the following rule which, according to Festus (ed. Lindsay, 505), originated with Numa Pompilius and was intended to protect the boundaries separating the fields: *Numa Pompilius statuit eum qui terminum exarassit et ipsum et boves sacros esse.* 'Numa Pompilius decided that whoever dug up the boundary line of a field while ploughing would be offered up to the gods of the underworld along with his animals.' Boundary lines had a sacred character. To disturb them was to commit an act of sacrilege in a primitive society. Hence, the guilty party who exposed the city to the risk of divine anger was declared *sacer* and could be killed by any citizen.

Roman law, known to the pontiffs only, remained unwritten until the middle of the fifth century when it was set down and published for the first time; a code prepared by a decemviral commission was engraved on twelve tables and from this it took its name, *Laws of the XII Tables.* There has been much argument as to the exact date of this first publication of the Roman law, although there can be no doubt as to that given in the traditional account, even if the surviving fragments had been retouched and brought up to date at the end of the Republic and beginning of the Empire. Many legal systems known to us are analogous with the so-called Royal Laws. Thus the supreme curse, the *sacer esto*, is laid on the *patronus* who has injured his client: '*Patronus si clienti fraudem fecerit sacer esto.*' Similarly, Pliny the Elder writes that a man stealing crops is to be killed to satisfy Ceres (*Natural History*, XVIII, 12): in other words, the State undertook the punishment but it remained a peace-offering to the divinity offended by a sacrilegious act.

The word *sacer* gave rise to a series of ideas and terms which were extremely important in the religious life of Rome; there was *sacrare*, to consecrate; the compound *consecrare*, with the same meaning; *exsecrare*, to execrate, curse; *obsecrare*, to pray in the name of the gods. *Sacrificare* came from *sacrum facere*, meaning first, to perform a sacred ceremony, then to sacrifice. From *sacrare* a series of key-nouns in Roman religion and law were derived. The *sacramentum* was the lodgement of a certain sum of money with the gods as a guarantee of one's good faith or the justice of one's cause. As this lodgement was accompanied by the taking of an oath, the word *sacramentum* itself took on the meaning of sacrament. The *sacerdos* was the man who performed sacred ceremonies, or priest, the *sacrilegus* was the man who stole sacred objects, or sacrilegious person. The adjective *sanctus*, derived from *sancire* and belonging to the same root as *sacer*, meant literally 'made sacred', 'inviolable', and was to have an unforeseen success in the Latin and Romance languages of the Christian era.

Is it possible to discover in the early Roman citizen a feeling for the sacred, for the presence of those forces alternating between benevolence and malevolence which take man into a world beyond his own? For this it is necessary to envisage his reactions in the face of many phenomena which he did not understand and in which he saw prodigies, and his feelings when entering desolate places, the deep woods where man has often felt himself in contact with forces dominating him. From the beginning the interpretation and expiation of prodigies was important in the life of the dwellers on the seven hills, as is evidenced by the detailed manner in which, under the Republic, the consuls listed to the Senate all the prodigies that had been seen, year by year; whereupon the Senate had them expiated by the highest Roman religious authorities. In the face of such prodigies and the traces they left in the world, the Roman felt a sacred thrill, for they represented to his eyes the concrete, awful sign of the intervention on earth of invisible forces which governed man's fate. The unnatural phenomena announced at Rome aroused a sort of religious horror, which survives in many passages of Livy's history.

The same feeling of *horror*, the same sacred thrill, possessed the Roman when he entered the sacred woods, the *luci* or *nemora*, which had been the focal-points of religion and venera-tion in Rome and the surrounding area from the very beginning. The vegetation on the Roman hills themselves had also aroused a certain religious interest, from which sprang the names of 'Viminal', meaning 'hill of willows', and 'Fagutal', 'hill of beeches'. As aforementioned, one of the oldest of Rome's holy spots was the asylum created by Romulus on the Capitol as a refuge for exiled or banished men. This asylum was situated between two sacred woods, *inter duos lucos*, and there is little doubt that this fact constituted an effective magical safeguard.

These sacred woods belonged to and were lived in by divini-ties who were anonymous at the beginning but later took on clearly defined identities and names. Numa Pompilius's meet-ings with the goddess Egeria took place, according to Livy (I, 21), in a sacred wood, a *lucus*, in the middle of which there was a dark grotto whence sprang an inexhaustible spring. As Numa often went there alone, in order to meet the goddess, he dedicated the wood to the Muses, saying that he met them there with his wife Egeria. Like woods, springs also had a mysterious and sacred quality, and both in Rome and in Italy in general there were many beneficent goddesses presiding over various *fontes*. Spring-worship can be seen in many primitive cultures, and is an expression of the profound and deeply rooted religious feeling that we are trying to analyse in the Rome of the first centuries. It was not until the beginning of the Christian era that writers such as Seneca gave expression to an intimation of divinity to be felt in the solitude of the forest (combined in Seneca's case, with reflections on the sacred character of the soul and a vague spirituality stemming from the ideas of the period, and his own philosophical views). But this same fore-boding goes back directly to the old Latin cults of the forest-gods and the *horror* stimulated in the earliest Romans by the mysterious appearance of the *nemus*. There is, for example, this passage by Seneca in his *Letters to Lucilius* (XLI, 1–4): 'If you find a sacred forest crowded with old trees of great height with branches which with their layers of foliage block out the sky, the vigour of this arboreal growth, the mystery of the place, the density of this shadow in the midst of open country imbues you with the idea of divine power.' Finally, everything to do with the next world belonged to the sphere of the sacred and untouchable; above all, graves and tombs were inviolable, protected by supernatural powers. The cult of the dead was to play an important part throughout the religious history of Rome. In the classical period the huge body of sacred things, ceremonies and feelings was divided, on the legal level, into three distinct categories, the *res sacrae* belonging to the gods above after their consecration by the pontiffs, the *res religiosae*, identifiable as the graves, the property of the gods of the underworld and ruled by a very rigorous code of law, and lastly the *res sanctae*, which were things placed under the protection of the gods by a ritual ceremony, such as the walls and gates of Rome. This artificial distinction, however, did not alter the fact that at the beginning these different categories shared a common feeling of religious respect and prohibition.

Besides these basic facts about religious feeling in Rome, recent research has revealed much information regarding the birth and evolution of certain important rites and practices in Rome under royal rule. The Latin tribes on the Alban hills were linked by common religions dedicated to Jupiter *Latiaris* and Diana of Aricia. These two divinities were worshipped in sanctuaries with a federal importance, Jupiter on the top of Monte Cavo (*Mons Latiaris*), Diana by the calm, soothing Lake of Nemi. Alba Longa apparently founded the sanctuary of Monte Cavo, Aricia that of Diana of Nemi, whose archaic and magical quality has long attracted the attention of modern sociologists. For a long time Rome shared in the ceremonies which united the peoples of Latium. It was not until the end of the royal period that she was in a position to assert herself as a new religious capital, a leader in her own right. A temple, founded according to tradition by Servius Tullius and dedi-cated to Diana, was built on the Aventine; the Romans intended it to supplant the old sanctuary of the Alban hills and deliberately chose as its foundation date August 13, which was the date of the feast of Aricia. At about the same period, Rome re-adopted the cult of Jupiter *Latiaris* and itself organized an annual sacrifice of a white bull, during the *Feriae Latinae*, which marked the date of the truce.

The cult-connexions between Rome and the rest of Latium were not limited to the city's annexation of the federal cults. The religious life of Latin cities such as Lavinium, Lanuvium, Aricia, Tusculum, Ardea and others was very active during the whole of the period of the Roman kings and persisted even when these cities had become completely unimportant. Now, Rome was always open to religious influences from its neigh-bours, whether friendly or unfriendly. Consequently, many cults belonging to Latin cities were also acknowledged, one after another, in Rome. Sometimes they were amicably shared. Juno Sospita had two abodes, Rome and Lanuvium, her place of origin. Every year the ancient town of Lavinium was visited by Roman praetors, consuls and dictators who came to sacrifice to Vesta and the Penates when their term of office either began or ended. This did not prevent Rome from simultaneously doing honour to the public Penates in the city itself and thus worshipping the same gods twice over.

Plate 60

The *evocatio*, historically attested on several occasions during the life of the Roman republic, was a very ancient ritual in which the Roman general invited the tutelary divinities of the city he was besieging to leave their homes and to take up residence in Rome where temples more worthy of them would be built for them. This ritual is a particularly striking example of the tolerance, not to say open-mindedness, of the Roman religious consciousness with regard to foreign gods. It has justly been compared with an analogous rite practised from the second millennium B.C. by the Hittites, a people of Indo-European origin inhabiting the centre of Asia Minor. The rite was certainly an Indo-European idea, totally opposed to the outlook of the Semitic peoples who made war not only on their enemies but also on their enemies' gods. In the Semitic east a god was conquered with his people and forced to perish or go into bondage along with his worshippers.

Like the gods acquired peaceably, those 'evoked' from enemy cities were romanized after entering the *Urbs*. Their names were latinized, and there was frequently an assimilation-process, the *interpretatio romana*, between the foreign god and a divinity already worshipped in Rome. To the Roman mind the difference in name between gods from different places concealed a deep-seated similarity between the gods themselves which extended across all the different religions of ancient Italy.

In his *Saturnalia* (III, 9) Macrobius gives valuable information as to the detail of the *evocatio*. It took place, he says, when the Romans did not think it possible to capture the enemy city in any other way. But in any case they would have thought it sacrilege to take gods prisoner. On the contrary, they needed to take certain precautions to avoid receiving such treatment from their enemies. Therefore the deity who protected the *Urbs Roma* and the Latin name of the *Urbs* were jealously kept secret. One of the plebeian tribunes, Valerius Soranus, a boyhood friend of Varro's, underwent the supreme punishment for having transgressed the sacred, inflexible rule of silence. The *evocatio* consisted essentially of an incantatory formula pronounced by the leader of the forces at the time of the assault on a besieged town; this formula promised the enemy gods temples more worthy of them if they consented to go over to Rome. It was therefore a *votum publicum* containing detailed promises of recompense if the prayer was answered. But behind this ritual, despite all the formulae of deference and respect, one senses a threat of force which verges on the sphere of primitive magic. The name in question, as in every incantation, possessed powers of its own.

In 496 B.C. the Roman legions were involved in a severe battle with a coalition of Latin troops. In the thick of the fighting, the Roman dictator Aulus Postumius promised a temple to Castor, a Greek hero, who along with his brother Pollux had become the tutelary deity of Tusculum. As soon as the victory was complete and a treaty of alliance had been concluded with the Latins, Rome received Castor and Pollux on to her territory, although it is true that they continued to be worshipped in Tusculum. They became the patrons of the Roman cavalry, and in 484 a temple was dedicated to them in the heart of the Forum. But afterwards the *evocatio*, in the strict sense of the word, was used only in the most important wars: in 386 Juno Regina left Veii at the moment of the decisive

Fig. 21

assault on the town; in 264 Vertumnus, the main god of the Volsinii, left them for Rome in the same way; and in 146 Carthage was only finally destroyed after having been ritually stripped of all divine aid.

Thus Rome's religious life developed in a sort of symbiotic relationship to her sister cities in Latium; there was not only much reciprocal borrowing but also a series of parallel develop/ ments of elements of worship stemming from a common heri/ tage. There thus arose in Rome a number of cults and rituals that were undoubtedly very ancient, although they are difficult to date exactly. Nevertheless, it is possible to make out some kind of chronological scheme. The beginnings and progressive extension of the city explain the setting of the ceremonies and feasts, why they took place in such and such a part of the hills or valleys. The Palatine rituals, the *Palilia*, celebrated on April 21 and the *Lupercalia* on February 15, were held by the Romans to be older than the foundation of the city itself. This association with remote antiquity cannot be dismissed as com/ pletely unfounded. On the contrary, it is certain that these feasts, which retained their primitive, magical character and which were dedicated respectively to the fertility of all livestock on the Palatine Hill and to the safeguarding of the spot, were insti/ tuted by the first occupants of the Palatine, shortly after their arrival in the eighth century B.C.

Two valleys gradually became the religious centres of Rome, and they contained from a very early date various important cults. The Forum gradually took first place in religious life and became its centre and core. Ancient taboos were attached to certain parts of it, and these came to be embodied in legends and tales; there was, for instance, the site of a sacred tree (the Volcanal, at the foot of the Capitol), and the place reserved for sacrifices to the dead, the *Lacus Curtius*, where originally, perhaps, the sacrificial offerings were human beings.

In the historical period human sacrifices became the exception,

Fig. 4

and Rome had recourse to them only in the greatest crises, as for instance during the second Punic War when twice, on the order of the Senate who were following the prescriptions of the Sibylline Books, two couples of Gauls and Greeks were buried alive on the Forum Boarium. But mostly the Roman gods were content with substitute sacrifices, the best known being that of the Argei. Every year the pontiffs and Vestals hurled twenty-seven to thirty rush-figures, called Argei, down from the Pons Sublicius into the Tiber: this was a survival of certain human sacrifices to chthonian deities.

A peculiar form of human sacrifice did, however, survive in the rite of the *devotio*, which is attested only three times, in 340, 295 and 279, but which in fact dated back to the remote past. According to this rite three members of the famous *gens* of the Decii offered themselves up to the gods to save their city. We know the details of these voluntary sacrifices from certain extremely useful passages in Livy's *Histories* (Chapters 9 to 10 of Book VIII), which recall the sacred rules of the primitive ritual and describe the *devotio* of the consul Decius in 340 during a hard battle between Roman and Latin troops which took place not far from Vesuvius. Seeing that his left wing was yielding before the enemy, Decius decided to 'devote' himself for his legions. A pontiff who was present guided him as to the attitude he should assume. He made him put on the *toga praetexta*, veil his head and recite, standing on a javelin placed on the ground, a ritual formula which began with an invoca-tion embracing the whole of the Roman pantheon. The consul vowed his life to the gods of the earth and the underworld, the Manes and Tellus, in exchange for the salvation of his army. But while offering up himself he also offered the enemy armies to the Manes and Tellus. After reciting the prayer, Decius, armed and on horse-back, leapt into the ranks of the opposing army; transfigured by the magic rite he appeared superhuman, an envoy from the gods charged to expiate their anger and to divert the menacing danger from his own forces to the enemy. At sight of him the Latins were terrified and fled.

The *devotus* could be either one of the generals of the Roman army or a plain soldier whom a general had chosen. If he did not die the rite was considered not to have been properly fulfilled, and the gods had to be appeased by sacrifices and substitute-offerings. In reality the *devotus* became a sort of spreading plague, as Livy indicates when he calls it a *pestis*. If the *devotus* escaped death, sacred acts of the greatest importance were required to purify him. If he was a soldier a statue at least seven feet tall had to be buried and a sacrifice made. No Roman magistrate was allowed to pass over the spot where the statue was buried. If the *devotus* was a general he made no public or private sacrifice, but offered up all his weapons to Vulcan or another god. It was a sacrilege for the enemy to gain possession of the javelin on which the consul had stood when making his *devotio*. If the enemy did get hold of it, a special expiatory sacrifice, the *suovetaurilia*, had to be made to Mars. The essence of this archaic rite, therefore, was that during the *devotio* all the good influences of the general passed into the *telum* under his feet while he drew down upon himself and his own personal weapons all the evil influences menacing his troops, and then passed over these influences to the enemy.

Plate 4

When the villages on the different hills formed themselves into a single city their respective religions, originally quite distinct, were grouped together in the Forum. From that time a perpetual flame burned in the circular temple of Vesta. Close by, the building known as the *Regia*, which was the abode of the *Rex*, a religious head and priest of Janus, was a concrete symbol of the religious unity of the city. The two buildings contained precious talismans, guaranteeing the survival and prosperity of Rome. The lances of Mars, the god of war, were piously preserved in one of the chapels of the *Regia*.

Plate 10

The broad valley stretching between the Palatine and the

133

Aventine was excluded, by reason of its slightly more remote position, from the Roman religious system. But from an early date ancient agrarian divinities of a Latin, or more generally Italic type, were grouped in this area. In it were worshipped the patron goddesses of cereal crops and harvests, such as Seia, Segetia and Tutilina. There was an underground altar to the god Consus, apparently the god of silos, protector of planted corn. According to tradition it was in honour of Consus that Romulus founded the biannual feasts and games, the *Consualia*, celebrated in the *Vallis Murcia*. An ancient magical bond linked the *ludi*, games of equestrian origin, with the agrarian cults. The races and competitions promoted the activity of the powers of the underworld and were an excellent means of assuring the fertility of the soil, exalting the valour of warriors and making certain of the satisfaction of the dead. The horse races, which had taken place between the Palatine and the Aventine from the time of the first kings, led to the building of the *Circus Maximus*, whose tiers were laid out by Tarquinius Superbus. The Etruscan tyrants extended the games, which dated back to the very origins of the city. The building in 493 of a triple temple dedicated to the fertility gods, Ceres, Liber and Libera, added to the number of agrarian divinities present in the *Circus Maximus* area.

To get a complete picture of the many primitive ceremonies performed in the Rome of the first centuries, one must investigate the archaic rituals which owed their survival to Roman conservatism, even if they were sometimes diverted from their original functions. The strange gesticulations performed twice a year in different parts of the town by the Salians, or dancing priests, are perhaps the best example of ceremonies about which we now have accurate information; by collating the results of archaeological and sociological research with textual material it is possible to distinguish their exact origin and the develop-ment of their character through the ages.

Tradition gives varying accounts of the origin of the Salians; here, however, are a few of the basic accepted facts. Their birth and sacred mission in Rome stemmed from the fall of a sacred bronze shield, the *ancile*, out of the heavens. During an epidemic that was devastating the city a shield of a shape unusual in Italy—it had an indentation in each of the long sides of the oval—fell into the hands of King Numa Pompilius. Shortly afterwards the plague ceased. Numa, the archetype of the pious king, immediately pronounced that the object which had fallen out of the sky was a pledge of the future happiness and prosperity of Rome. To prevent robbery he commanded a smith called Mamurius Veturius to make eleven shields exactly like the first one. The twelve shields, including the most sacred, the *pignus imperii,* were entrusted to the care of a religious brotherhood created for the purpose, the Salians. These were to keep the *ancilia* in a sacred building on the Palatine, the *curia Saliorum.* In the same sanctuary were placed the statue of Mars armed with a lance and Romulus's augural staff, or *lituus,* the instrument essential to the foundation of Rome. As guardians of the sacred arms, the Salians of the Palatine acted as servants of Mars *gradivus,* the god of war. A second brotherhood of Salians, those of the Quirinal, was later created by King Tullus Hostilius, but in very different circum-stances. During a difficult battle against the Sabines, Tullus swore to institute a second Salian brotherhood if he won the battle that very day. When this came to pass he fulfilled his promise and created a brotherhood of twelve Salians dedicated to the cult of the god Quirinus. They were never as important as their colleagues on the Palatine.

Every year the Salian brotherhoods performed ceremonies consisting of warlike dances which celebrated the beginning and end of the war season. In March they 'moved the *ancilia*', according to the sacred phrase, *ancilia movere.* This meant that they danced through the town, stopping at various places where, led by their master, or *magister*, the leading dancer, or *praesul*, and a cantor, or *vates*, they leapt about to a ternary rhythm while striking the *ancilia* with a short lance and singing prayers of invocation to various gods. Then they took part in the horse races known as the *Equirria* on March 14, and ensured the lustration of weapons on the 19th. Corresponding with these rites celebrating the opening of the war season there were similar ones in October to celebrate the end of the season. The *ancilia* were then deposited in the *sacrarium* (*ancilia condere*).

This was how the Ancients envisaged this sodality. Behind the rational part of the account there is to be found a bed-rock of primordial beliefs: a regular cycle of dances using the arms with the divine imprint upon them; rites of a very early date confirmed, as we shall see, by archaeological evidence.

The armed dance with the *ancilia* was not peculiar to Rome; Alba, Lavinium, Tusculum, Tibur and Agnani all possessed their own brotherhoods of Salians from a very early period. In his *Commentary on the Aeneid* (VII, 285) Servius goes so far as to state that the peoples of Tibur and Tusculum had their Salians before the Romans. The oval shield with indentations on two sides was not a sacred weapon at Rome only. *Juno Sospita* of Lanuvium, a war goddess, brandished a lance with her right hand and held an *ancile* with her left. Cicero, in his *De Natura Deorum* (I, 29, 83), describes her *ancile* as a

Plate 60

scutulum, a small oval shield. But the many portraits of the goddess leave us in no doubt as to the exact form of the shield; it was the same as the sacred *ancile* of the Salians.

The Ancients give information not only as to the existence of a cycle of Salian dances at Rome but also as to the actual character of the dances performed. They were composed of three elements, all blended into one rhythm: the steps, the singing and the sound of the lances striking the shields. The terms describing the steps—*saltatio* and *tripudium*—allude to a heavy, regular beat in ternary rhythm. It had none of the grace or beauty of ordinary dance movements, so that the priestly function was open to the common man, who needed no particular talent. All the same, the ceremonies performed by the college constituted a fairly strenuous athletic training; Seneca in his *Letters to Lucilius* (XV, 4) quotes as one of the relatively easy physical exercises, which nevertheless develop the body,

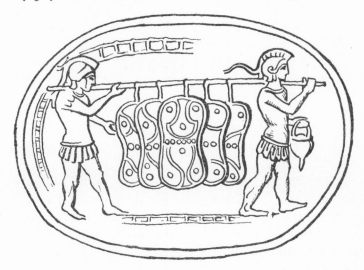

Fig. 20   Scene engraved on a cornelian intaglio showing two men in military uniform carrying five ancilia *hung on a pole. Apparently these are not the Salian priests carrying their own sacred shields, as on the older intaglio shown in pl. 59, but their servants in soldiers' dress. cf. A. Furtwängler, Die antiken Gemmen, Pl. xxii, no. 62. About 8:1*

the series of jumps repeated on the spot, after the manner of the Salians. This exercise, according to Catullus (XVII, 1), was sufficient to endanger bridges which were not in perfect condition. The hymn sung by the Salians was so archaic that they themselves had difficulty in understanding its meaning, according to Quintilian.

Two questions are of particular interest. What were the origins of the sacred army of the Salians, and what was the

Plate 59

Fig. 20

original value of their dance? There are no *ancilia* still in existence, but the descriptions by classical writers, together with various pictures, gems, coins and bas-reliefs showing either the ceremony of the moving of the *ancilia* by the Salians or the weapon alone, show us exactly what it looked like; it was a large oval shield with a wide indentation on both its long sides. The only comparable objects from Italic territory known to us are small bronze plaques, roughly oval and with indentations on the short sides. They were votive shields or, in one case, a shield intended for use in dancing. These interesting objects come from Picenum, the *ager capenas*, and from Bolsena. They all date from the Early Iron Age; more exactly, from about 700 B.C. and the succeeding period. Their siting on Italian territory tells us a great deal and enables us, in my opinion, to retrace the route taken by this unusual type of weapon on its way to Latium and Rome itself.

The ultimate origin of this form of shield is to be found in the Cretan and Mycenaean cultures, which left many pictures of characteristic large shields, called figure-of-eight shields. From these developed the shield with deep indentations found in Greece in the geometrical period, a type of weapon portrayed on Dipylon vases; such shields, used as votive objects, have been found in various parts of Greece, at Olympia and in the temple of Athena at Tegea, and they served as a model for the indented shields made by the Italic peoples. No doubt the form crossed the Adriatic after passing through Illyria. Picenum was linked to the *ager capenas* by numerous currents of influences. From Capena it was easy for trends to reach the various cities in Latium. Varying adaptations of the common prototype account for the different placing of the indentations. The strangeness of the form explains why the Latin towns regarded it as sacred and bearing the stamp of divinity. It was not unusual for primitive peoples to confuse the exotic with the sacred. Out of this grew the Roman legend of the *ancile* which fell out of the sky. The date of the archaeological evidence found in certain parts of Italy agrees with that attri-buted by the Roman historians to this mythical episode and confirms that the *ancile* appeared in Rome in about 700.

But better even than this: by chance an exceptional piece of archaeological evidence has survived which represents a scene from the armed dance as it was performed at the beginning of the eighth century, on the border between Latium and Etruria. This is a bronze biconical urn found in a grave in Bisenzio on the west side of the lake of Bolsena. On its shoulders and lid there is depicted a curious scene comprising a group of several figurines executed in a primitive and awkward style. On two concentric circles are naked warriors wearing only a flat head-dress and performing a sort of dance in which they gesticulate and flourish lances and small round shields. Some of them carry shields in both hands. They are grouped round a four-footed animal, possibly a bear, which is attached to the centre of the lid. Among the armed dancers is a character who is pushing forward a cow which another character appears to be about to sacrifice. The minute size of the figurines and the awkwardness of the still undeveloped technique prevent a detailed analysis of the complex scene shown. It is clear, how-ever, that it is meant to depict a magical dance. Judging from the circles of dancers, the dance and the noisy clashing of weapons round the chained animal, this performance was probably meant to ensure luck in the chase and also to protect men and flocks against wild beasts.

Plate 58

This raises the question of the original significance of the Salian dances that were beginning to be performed in various towns in Latium at the same period. Everything leads to the conclusion that they were a sort of mime of war, intended by means of imitative magic to ensure the success of Rome and the downfall of her enemies in military campaigns. But many ethnologists, such as Sir James Frazer in his *Commentary on the*

Fasti of Ovid, believe that the primitive origin of these rites is different, more broadly based. They accept that the violent sounds made by the repeated clashing of the metal shields and all the war-mime were meant as a means of ensuring victory, but claim that the enemies in question were neither individuals nor whole peoples but the beings most feared by primitive men —the evil spirits who were always on the watch, a constant danger menacing the tribe. The armed dance was to protect the tribe, its prosperity, the fertility of its flocks and crops. It still seems to be a matter of choice whether one envisages the performance as a war-rite or an agrarian purification rite.

The Salians were the priests of Mars; but this is not conclusive proof of the character of their dances. For, although from the beginning Mars was a war god rather than the agrarian type of god suggested by some scholars, he made war not only after the fashion of men but also against evil spirits when they threatened peasants and their crops.

In my opinion, a question of development at a very early date is involved. A distinction must be made between the original meaning of the rite and the meaning that it swiftly acquired within the growing system of the Roman religion. Comparisons between the Latin armed dances and the apotropaic dances performed by many primitive peoples appear to be conclusive. Take, for example, the description by Apollonius of Rhodes of the armed dances instituted on the advice of Orpheus, after the Argonauts had involuntarily slaughtered the king of Cyzicus and his people, their hosts of the previous night: 'At the same time, on the advice of Orpheus, the young men leaped in time, dancing the armed dance. They struck their shields with the swords, in order to drive away the laments of evil omen which the people were still uttering for the death of the king.' (*Argonautica*, I, line 1134 and ff.) Immediately, a spring rose on a hill-top which had hitherto been completely arid. These first corybantic dances thus appear to have been for apotropaic and fertility purposes. Comparisons of this sort leave no doubt as to the analogous character of the Salian dances at their beginnings. And the valuable evidence of the vase of Bisenzio, showing the magical dance, confirms this view.

But very soon, probably from the first half of the seventh century, the Roman cult incorporated these dances into a regular, ordered cycle; they became ceremonies of military consecration and deconsecration, solemnities giving a precise rhythm to warfare. Soon the military quality was the only one that lived on in Roman consciousness. This regularization of rites originally far more archaic and complex in meaning is in line with one of the deepest-rooted tendencies of Roman religion. The aim was always to organize its various feasts and fasts into a precise scheme.

Turning from the ancient magic rituals to the gods, one finds an unusually complex religious panorama. It is true that the literary evidence at our disposal concerns relatively late periods. But the Roman historians assigned the first over-all organization of the State's religion to the Sabine King Numa Pompilius. A calendar engraved on stone, which was discovered in Anzio, lists the holy days and ancient feasts (in large capitals) side by side with various dates and religious anniversaries (in smaller letters). It evidently represents an ancient calendar, pre-Republican but not as early as the eighth century. It dates from the end of the Etruscan monarchy, probably from the second half of the sixth century.

Thus there are indications of attempts at systematic organization from an early date. This was necessitated by the gradual multiplication of the cults. The number of Roman gods seems to have been very large from the outset, and it is difficult to discern their origins. At first they were personal forces but not in human form. Apparently anthropomorphism was not natural to the Latins, who lacked visual imagination and did not easily create myths and legends. They addressed divinities indifferently as of either sex—*sive deus, sive dea*. To their minds the world presented itself as a network of *numina* presiding over the natural cycles and men's actions. The invocations to the gods (each addressed by his own name), virtual litanies called *indigitamenta*, brought the various stages of a single human action or of a single crop-growth under the protection of various divinities. One after another, *Vaticanus, Cumina, Ruminus* or *Rumina, Statilinus, Abeona* and *Adeona* watched over the various stages of the child's growth, his cradle, his milk, his first steps, his first words. The patron goddess of the corn in seed form was *Seia*; when it was above the ground it came under the protection of *Segetia*, and when it was gathered and stored it was watched over by *Tutilina* (Saint Augustine, *The City of God*, IV, 8).

Rome's religious psychology thus reflected a pragmatical attitude, a concern with practical affairs that was one of its most deeply-rooted characteristics. The same trait can be seen in Roman methods of divination, in their ways of interpreting the signs given by the gods. Compared with the extreme ingenuity shown by the Greeks and Etruscans in making out the lines of the near or distant future, the Roman attitude is quite different. The Romans constantly consulted the gods, but not about their future. They confined themselves to asking simple questions about the possibilities of enterprises already under way. They read the answers in the words uttered, *omina*, and the various flights of the birds, *auspicia*. But so that they should not be hampered by all these omens, they invented a whole series of loopholes for not paying attention to them. Augural law thus became a system of casuistry, preserving liberty of action. It will be remembered that the inscription in the *Lapis Niger* contains one of those prudent rules which, to avoid evil omens, is so phrased as to exclude the possibility of any being seen.

Fig. 22

In his religious life, therefore, the Roman thought and practised as a man of action. His interest in the present and the well-being of both the individual and the State made him constantly strive after the *pax Deorum*, or peace with the gods, on which depended his own future and that of the city. The rites and ceremonies of traditional religion helped to maintain this tacit alliance. But such a *status quo* was a truce rather than a real peace; it was under the constant threat of disruption if the gods were insulted by some lack of devotion in the homage paid to them. Then would come a prodigy, an irruption of the sacred into the non-sacred world; for the gods, benevolent if satisfied, were terrible if their laws were infringed. At such a time the city and its occupants stood in the midst of perils, and neither the human heart nor the town could find peace until expiatory ceremonies, *procurationes prodigiorum*, restored the old balance.

It must not be forgotten, of course, that the receptivity of the Latin and Roman religions towards foreign cults meant that they were influenced from an early date by the Greek religion and that of the Etruscans. Long before the large-scale Hellenization of the Roman cults after the Punic Wars at the end of the third century B.C., there had already been a gradual influx of Greek gods and rites, either direct from Magna Graecia or through Etruria. It is not easy to analyse this Hellenic influence with regard to the earliest periods in Rome, much less to isolate the Etruscan factors. Nevertheless, their importance must not be exaggerated, although the Romans' commercial links with Greek territories, the artistic influence from the Greeks and the presence of the Etruscans who deepened the impact of the first two factors, certainly accustomed them to the personalities of the Greek gods. For a hundred and seventy years, according to Varro, they had no statues of their own gods, but eventually Etrusco-Greek statuary accustomed them to an anthropo-morphism which did not come naturally to them. From the royal period, Greek gods were adopted by various more or less

Etruscanized Latin cities and from these they often progressed to Rome. This phenomenon seems to have reached its height at the end of the Etruscan period of Roman history. In 496 Aulus Postumius swore an oath to the Dioscuri of Tusculum where they were worshipped; in 484 a temple to them was built in the Forum itself. The temple of Mercury, outside the *pomoerium* behind the Porta Capena, dates from 484: Mercury can be identified with the Greek god Hermes who was adopted by the Etruscans under the name of Turms. Hercules, who was very popular with the Etruscans under the name of Hercle, seems, however, to have come to Rome direct from Magna Graecia.

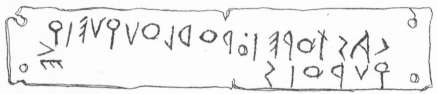

Fig. 21   *Archaic dedication to Castor and Pollux recently found at Lavinium. It is engraved on a bronze lamella 11⅜ in. long, 2 in. wide and ⁸⁄₄ in. to ₁⁄₁₆ in. thick. This drawing is taken from that reproduced in an article by Professore Castagnoli. 'Dedica arcaica lavinate a Castore e Polluce', in* Studi e Materiali di Storia delle Religioni, *1959, xxx, 1*

Fig. 21

With regard to the Dioscuri, a new archaic inscription has just been discovered at Lavinium and its recent publication has contributed much to our knowledge. The inscription in question is engraved on a short bronze lamella and the writing used proves that the text dates from a very early period, probably about the same as the inscription on the cippus of the Forum (end of the sixth to beginning of the fifth century B.C.).

The text, which is very short, is a dedication as follows: *Castorei Podlouqueique qurois.* The morphological anomalies are considerable. It is hard to account for the form *Podlouquei,* meaning 'to Pollux'. On the one hand, the letter-combination 'dl' existed neither in Latin nor in the Italic languages; on the other hand, the labio-velar which ends the name 'Pollux' is very strange. *Qurois* is no less puzzling. It is a unique case, applying purely and simply to the Greek *kouroi*. The Latin inscription is modelled upon a Greek dedication.

As it stands, the dedication shows no Etruscan influence whatever. At Lavinium the two heroes were worshipped with their purely Greek characteristics almost from the time of their introduction to Rome.

The influence of Greece and Etruria is clearly to be seen in the difficult question of the origin of the mysterious Sibylline books, which were to become gradually more and more important to the religious life of Rome. It was said that an old woman, the Sybil of Cumae, offered to sell certain books containing her own oracles to one of the Etruscan kings of Rome; Tarquin the Elder, according to some, Tarquinius Superbus, according to others. Exasperated by the refusal of her offer, she burned several of them and the monarch, impressed by this, bought the remaining books. Two priests, the *Duoviri Sacris faciundis*, whose number was later increased to ten and then fifteen, were created to consult and interpret them as and when the Senate required. When, early in the second half of the fifth century, the god Apollo was introduced into Rome, he became the patron of the sacred writings, and they played a large part in the adoption of the Greek cult in Rome.

But the Ancients themselves did not recognize the existence of a collection of Cumaean oracles. And from the material in them are reproduced by Roman historians, the books seem at the beginning to have been sacred rules for warding off the most menacing prodigies, rather than oracles. The origin of these rules appears to have been complex, partly Greek, partly Etruscan, partly Latin. The traditional story can, no doubt, be partially explained by the later transformation of the books, which from the third century took on a new character and absorbed certain real prophecies. But there is no doubt that the collection was first made in the period of the Etruscan kings. The obscurity of the legendary account is, no doubt, traceable to the vagueness of the Romans when dealing with a period of mixed cultures, Etruscan and Greek.

The purely Etruscan element in the religion of Rome remained small. The theological thinking of the Etruscans was too remote from the Latins' religious outlook to make a lasting impression on it. Nevertheless, the framework of the Etruscan religion left its mark on the organization of the Roman calendar and on the hierarchies of certain cults; and the specialized group of Etruscan diviners, undisputed masters of the art of divination, constituted the last resort of the Senate when especially terrifying prodigies demanded new and unknown ceremonies for their expiation.

Two sanctuaries built by the Etruscans were to remain as evidence of the growing imperialism in Rome at the end of the sixth century. These were the temple of Diana on the Aventine, which led to the amalgamation of the cults of various Latin peoples, and the Capitoline temple of Jupiter, *Optimus Maximus*, Juno and Minerva, which, long after the Etruscan period, remained the political and religious centre of Rome, and then of the countries subjugated by her. This, the first known grouping together of the chief god with the two goddesses, is an Etruscan innovation, as was also the trio of Ceres, Liber and Libera, to whom was built a threefold temple in the valley of the *Circus Maximus* at the beginning of the fifth century. The difficulties encountered by the author of a recent thesis[1] when he tried to explain this unusual grouping, seen nowhere else, are sufficient proof that it resulted from imitation of Etruscan cult habits. Threefold temples and cults were an essential element of the Etruscan religion. In the period from 496, when Aulus Postumius swore that he would build the temple, to 493, when it was consecrated, Rome was an Etruscan city and it was

[1] See Bibliography, p. 160 (Le Bonniec, H.).

Fig. 22 Bronze mirror from Vulci dating from the fourth century B.C. and now in the Etruscan Museum of the Vatican. The diviner Chalcas is examining the entrails of a sacrificial victim according to the usual practice of haruspication. cf. Gerhard, op. cit., II, p. 223

natural enough that a threefold temple, decorated by Greek artists and dedicated to divinities grouped according to the Etruscan system, should be built in it.

At the end of the royal period there was thus a large, complex and still increasing pantheon, which lacked, how' ever, any real theological structure. On the other hand a priestly order, hierarchically arranged, ensured the scrupulous performance of sacrifices and offerings, thus guaranteeing the success of the city's enterprises. A complex calendar minutely and methodically regulated the various cycles of annual feast, the war cycle, the cycle of crop fertility, of human and animal fertility and finally of death and purification. This religious structure of which ritualism and pragmatism were the basic elements, gradually became more complex during the follow' ing centuries. But it was not until the political and social upheavals and emotional shocks of the Punic Wars that new needs awoke in the Roman mind a desire for systems explaining the world and the fate of man. Until then the Romans remained content with a religion without any doctrine con' cerning the nature of the gods. For centuries, despite their gradual identification with Greek gods, these remained impersonal forces. Rituals existed in their own right, indepen' dent of all belief.

Conclusion

ANY SLICE taken out of the history of a city or people is bound to be artificial. For at no time are changes so abrupt that they turn completely away from the development preceding them. Nevertheless, the end of the royal period marks an important break in the history of Rome. Rich and powerful under the Tarquins, she had dominated Latium. The removal of the Etruscan armies reduced her to the rank of a Latin city of medium importance, threatened by the mountain peoples surrounding her, the Volsci, Hernici and Aequi, and forced to engage in bitter fighting to reconquer her newly lost hege⁄mony over the Latin plain. Her power and whole future destiny depended on the diligence of her farmers and the bravery of her soldiers. The fifth century was to be a difficult one, with Rome under constant threat from the poor primitive peoples of the central Apennines. A long period of austerity began, and art and luxury were not to reappear for a considerable time. Yet when conservative Romans like Cato expressed their horror at the influx into Rome of luxurious habits learned from the east, they forgot that several centuries earlier their ancestors had also eaten off gold and silver dishes.

In the political field the crisis which overtook Rome was not, as we now see, an isolated case. All central Italy underwent a similar experience. In Italy as in Rome, the State after the expulsion of the kings became a patrician one dominated by an oligarchy of *principes*. But while the social conditions of the Etruscan cities developed little, thereby leading to the revolts which occurred at the end of Etruscan history, the Roman *plebs* gradually evolved a real political identity and fought hard for an equality of rights. Changes in the military organization of the town are one of the principal causes of this. The early army relied mainly on the cavalry, recruited from the ranks of the nobles. From the Etruscan period, on account of the increase in expeditions and wars, a need was felt for a powerful infantry. It was the peasants, heavily armed as *hoplites,* who filled the ranks of the new phalanxes. And eventually after long and difficult struggles the *plebs,* who had re-entered the city, thanks to bold reforms of the Etruscan kings, obtained rights commen-surate with its duties.

Roman historians wrongly simplified this turning-point in Roman history. They envisaged the departure of the Tarquins as the end of a hated régime under which a single man ruled and all the citizens were enslaved. This hatred of monarchy was to become one of the leading ideas of Rome's internal policy. As the Romans saw it, tyrannical power and slavery (*dominatio* and *servitus*) ended in 509, and the State passed into the hands of the Roman people, its rightful owners. They came to feel an immense pride in the State's distant past, and from the very beginning the Republic took *libertas* as its watchword and motto. Half a millennium was to pass before power was once again represented by one single man, after the civil wars. But even then the title of 'king' was carefully avoided. The word 'liberty' retained its evocative power, and Augustus found it expedient to proclaim himself on his coins as *libertatis vindex,* saviour of liberty.

The above account has attempted to show how the primitive history of Rome now appears, taking into account the results obtained from various lines of research, and how facts have emerged from the shadowy regions of conjecture to which they were once confined. Neither the type of highly coloured history such as the Ancients wrote nor the personal and partly fictionalized theories of certain modern narrators are any longer justified. By means of archaeology, linguistics, epigraphy and comparative religious history it is possible to verify a large number of points and discern the broad outlines of cultural

evolution in the centuries once thought obscure. Some questions and problems naturally remain debatable. It is left to the
various fields of research, now well equipped for their task, to
continue the work which has been begun and to throw still
more light on the first years of the city that was to do more than
any other to influence the history of the west.

RECENT DEVELOPMENTS CONCERNING
THE STUDY OF ARCHAIC ROME

Archaeological exhibitions held recently in Rome make it easy
for us these days to view the most important excavations carried
out in Latium and on the site of archaic Rome. Since 30 August
1962, the prehistoric and protohistoric collections of Latium
(previously in the Museo Pigorini) have been displayed at the
Palazzo delle Scienze at the E.U.R. This 'Mostra delle Civiltà
preistoriche e protostoriche del Lazio' is very interesting and
instructive. Thanks to the efforts of our distinguished colleague,
M. Pietrangeli, the relics of archaic Rome are systematically
exhibited at the Palazzo Cafarelli in Rome. Particularly
striking is the display of Apennine pottery from the end of the
Bronze Age, found during the excavations at San Omobono.
The presence of Man on the site of Rome in the Bronze Age is
proved by various different archaeological discoveries, more or
less recent. It is therefore wise to remember M. Gjerstad's
significant observation: 'In any case the pre-urban epoch of
Rome has so far been extended into the first half of the second
millennium B.C. Another thing that becomes increasingly clear
is the fact that the earliest history of Rome forms an integral
part of that of Latium.'[1]

[1] E. Gjerstad, *Chalcolithic and Bronze Age Finds in Rome,* in 'Acta
Archaeologica', Vol. XXXII, Copenhagen, 1961, p. 1 ff.

Bibliography

The subject-matter treated in this book involves so many questions of such different kinds that there would be no practical value in a haphazard list of titles of books and articles. We prefer to link up these bibliographical notes with the different chapters to which they refer. In this way the reader will be able to turn to the works drawn on for the chapters he is actually reading and gain a systematic picture of the lines of research promoted by the origins of Rome.

Since CHAPTER I is purely an account of various scholarly approaches, we shall begin with the bibliography to CHAPTER II: *Peoples and Civilizations of Primitive Italy.*

CHAPTER II The following recently published methodical work will give an excellent idea of the large number of problems under consideration: 'Le origini storiche dei popoli italici' by M. PALLOTTINO in the *Relazioni del X Congresso Internationale di Scienze storiche*, II, Storia dell' Antichita, 1953, pp. 3 to 60. The same author has also written a concise article 'Popolazioni storiche dell'Italia antica', in *'Guida allo studio della Civiltà romana antica'*, I, pp. 4–20, Naples–Rome–Milan, 1952.

There are many works dealing with Indo–European migrations into Italy. We name only a few recent studies which themselves give biblio-graphies of earlier works: U. RELLINI, *Le origini della civiltà italica*, Rome, 1929; and 'Sulla civiltà dell'età enea in Italia' in the *Bollettino di Paletnologia Italiana*, LIII, 1933, pp. 63 ff. V. GORDON CHILDE, *Prehistoric Migrations in Europe*, Oslo, 1950. HUGH HENCKEN, 'Indo–European Languages and Archaeology' in the *American Anthropological Association*, LVII, no. 6, part 3, 84th transactions, December 1955. A general account of the archaeological evidence concerning Italian protohistory will be found in: G. KASCHNITZ–WEINBERG, 'Italien mit Sardinien, Sizilien und Malta', in *Handbuch der Archaologie*, II, I, Munich 1950, pp. 311 ff. See also, in connexion with graves, V. DUHN, FR. MESSERSCHMIDT, *Italische Gräberkunde*, Heidelberg, I, 1924; II, 1939.

The results of the stratigraphical excavations carried out on Ligurian territory and in the Aeolian islands give valuable information as to chronology. See: L. BERNABÒ BREA, *Gli scavi della caverna delle Arene candide*, Bordighera, I, 1946; II, 1956, and L. BERNABÒ BREA and M. CAVALIER, 'Civiltà preistoriche delle Isole eolie e del territorio di Milazzo', in the *Bollettino di Paletnologia Italiana*, LXV, 65, 1956, no. I, pp. 7–99.

A well documented general work on the so-called Apennine culture is now available. This is S. M. PUGLISI, *La Civiltà Apenninica. Origine delle communita pastorali in Italia*, Florence, 1959.

There are a large number of works dealing with Villanovan culture, which was so important at the beginning of the Etruscan and Latin cultures. Several of them were published a considerable time ago but have not been superseded as standard works. See: O. MONTELIUS, *La civilisation primitive en Italie*, 4 vols., Stockholm, 1895–1910; A. GRENIER, *Bologne villanovienne et étrusque*, Paris, 1912; D. RANDALL MacIVER, *Villanovans and Early Etruscans*, Oxford, 1924; P. DUCATI, *Storia di Bologna*, Bologna, 1928.

Of more recent works we quote only U. RELLINI, 'Sull' origine della civiltà del ferro in Italia' in *Studi etruschi*, XII, 1938, pp. 9 ff., and M. PALLOTTINO, *Sulle facies culturali arcaiche dell'Etruria*, I, XIII, 1939, pp. 85 ff. (main article). The low chronology in G. SÄFLUND, *Der geometrische Stil*, 1943, is debatable. There has recently been published an important book to which reference should be made: *Civiltà del Ferro: Studi pubblicati nella ricorrenza centenaria della scoperta di Villanova*, Bologna, 1959.

On various peoples and dialects of primitive Italy (apart from Latium) the following are important:

J. WHATMOUGH, *The Foundations of Roman Italy*, London, 1937.

On the Greeks: T. J. DUNBABIN, *The Western Greeks*, 1948; J. BÉRARD, *La colonisation grecque de l'Italie meridionale et de la Sicile dans l'Antiquité: l'histoire et la légende*, Paris, 2nd edition, 1957. B. PACE, *Arte e civiltà della Sicilia antica. I fattori etnici e sociali*, Rome-Milan, 1935.

On the Sardi: M. PALLOTTINO, *La Sardegna nuragica*, Rome, 1950.

On the Iapyges: M. MAYER, *Apulien*, Leipzig-Berlin, 1914.

On the Etruscans: M. PALLOTTINO, *L'origine degli Etruschi*, Rome, 1947. R. BLOCH, *The Etruscans*, London, 1958; the number of *Historia* devoted entirely to the Etruscans, VI, no. I, January 1957.

On the Falisci: L. ADAMS HOLLAND, 'The Faliscans in Prehistoric Times' in *Papers and Monographs of the American Academy in Rome*, VI, 1925.

The Origins of Rome

On the Osco-Umbrians: G. DEVOTO, _Gli antichi Italici_, 2nd edition, Florence, 1950.

On the Celts: H. HUBERT, _The Rise of the Celts_, London, 1934, and _The Greatness and Decline of the Celts_, London, 1934. T. G. E. POWELL, _The Celts_, London, 1958.

There are now many useful works on the Italic dialects: R. S. CONWAY, _The Italic Dialects_, Cambridge, 1897; R. VON PLANTA, _Grammatik des oskisch-umbrischen Dialekts_, Strassburg, 1892–7; C. D. BUCK, _A Grammar of Oscan and Umbrian_, Boston, 1904; G. DEVOTO, _Tabulae Iguvinae_, II, Rome, 1940; V. PISANI, _Le lingue d'Italia oltre il Latino_, Turin, 1953.

A number of articles recently published by M. PELLEGRINI in Italy and M. LEJEUNE in France, have added considerably to our knowledge of the Venetic language.

CHAPTER III The work by J. BÉRARD which has already been mentioned gives the documentation for the legends connected with the primitive peoples of Italy. However, despite the qualities of this excellent book and of its author, a personal friend and a great scholar whose early death is generally mourned, I cannot accept his theory of an actual precoloniza-tion, during the Mycenaean period, of many parts of Italy, and in particular Etruria and Latium. According to this view the legend of Aeneas would represent a re-telling of accurate historical facts. This is not confirmed by archaeological findings.

Les Origines de la légende troyenne by J. PERRET, on the other hand, gives the date attributed to the formation of the Aeneas legend as the third century B.C., after the expedition of Pyrrhus, King of Epirus, into Italy. This view is also contradicted by the archaeological evidence.

The whole question is discussed by F. BÖMER in _Rome und Troia, Untersuchungen zur Frühgeschichte Roms_, Baden-Baden, 1951, although we do not accept the book's daring conclusions as to the Roman penates. _Die trojanischen Urahnen der Römer_, by A. ALFÖLDI, Basle, 1957, is an interesting archaeological study confirming the importance of the Trojan legend in Etruria and Rome.

On the question of the legendary foundation of Ostia, see J. CARCO-PINO, _Virgile et les Origines d'Ostie_, Paris, 1919.

On the 'Romulean' sites in Classical Rome, see G. LUGLI, 'Il centro monumentale, _Roma Antica_, Rome, 1946.

There are an enormous number of works dealing with the Romulus legend and its importance in the formation of the Imperial mystique. The most important are: J. HUBAUX, *Les grands mythes de Rome*, Paris, 1945; J. GAGÉ, 'Romulus-Augustus' in *Mélanges de l'Ecole française de Rome*, 1930, pp. 138–81; J. CARCOPINO, *La louve du Capitole*, Paris, 1925; and several important archaeological articles by A. ALFÖLDI in *Museum Helveticum* from 1950 onwards.

On the monuments dating from the end of the first century B.C. and showing representations of the origins of Rome, see (for the frieze on the *Basilica Emilia*), A. BARTOLI, 'Il fregio figurato della Basilica Emilia', *Bollettino d'Arte*, XXXV, 1950, pp. 289–94, and (for the *Ara Pacis*) G. MORETTI, *Ara Pacis Augustae*, Rome, 1948.

G. DUMÉZIL has published the results of his work in comparative mythology in several books, e.g. *Mitra-Varuna: essai sur deux représentations indo-européennes de la souveraineté*, Bibliothèque des Hautes Etudes, LVI, 1940; *Jupiter, Mars et Quirinus*, Paris, 1941; *Horace et les Curiaces*, Paris, 1942; *Servius et la Fortune*, Paris, 1943; *Naissance de Rome (Jupiter, Mars et Quirinus*, II), Paris, 1949; *Les dieux des Indo-Européens*, Paris, 1951.

First, there is a good geographical study: J. LE GALL, *Le Tibre, fleuve de* CHAPTER IV *Rome, dans l'Antiquité*, Paris, 1951.

There is a vast literature on excavations of archaic Rome. Some of Boni's work is described in the numbers of *Notizie degli Scavi* for 1902, 1903, 1905, 1906, 1911, and Vaglieri's in the number for 1907. For excavations on the Capitol see A. M. COLINI, *Capitolium*, III, 1927; for those at Sant'Omobono, see the *Bollettino Communale*, LXVI, 1938. G. PINZA gives a useful account of the results obtained up to the date of his writing in 'Monumenti primitivi di Roma e del Lazio antico' in *Monumenti Ant.chi dei Lincei*, XVI, 1905.

In 'An archaeological record of Rome, from the seventh to the second century B.C.' in *Studies and Documents*, edited by Kirsopp Lake and Silva Lake, XIII, 2nd vol., London-Philadelphia, 1942, INEZ SCOTT RYBERG presents a synthesis of the results available in 1940 concerning the period mentioned in the title and thus excluding the beginnings of Rome. However, E. GJERSTAD is at present attempting a new synthesis, reviewing the archaeological evidence in the light of stratigraphical methods, under the title of *Early Rome*. Three volumes have already appeared: *Early*

Rome—I. Stratigraphical researches in the Forum Romanum and along the Via Sacra, Lund, 1956; *II. The Tombs*, Lund, 1956; *III. Fortifications, Domestic Architecture, Sanctuaries, Stratigraphic Excavations*, Lund, 1960 (in the series *Acta Instituti romani regni Sueciae*). The archaeological arguments used by Mr. Gjerstad are incontrovertible, although his conclusions as to chrono-logy in 'Scavi stratigrafici del Foro romano e problemi ad essi relativi' in the *Bollettino Communale di Roma*, LXXIII (1949–50), are arguable.

One work in particular is of supreme importance on the question of recent and early excavations in the Palatine settlements: S. M. PUGLISI's 'Gli abitatori primitivi del Palatino attraverso le testimonianze archeo-logiche e le nuove indagini stratigrafici sul Germalo', with additional chapters by P. ROMANELLI, A. DAVICO, G. DE ANGELIS D'OSSAT in *Monumenti Antichi dei Lincei*, XLI, 1951, pp. 1–146. We have drawn largely on this article in writing this book.

An account of the still controversial problems will be found in P. ROMANELLI, 'Problemi archeologichi del Foro Romano e del Palatino' in *Studi Romani*, I, January 1953. Some of the more recent discoveries are described in an article by P. ROMANELLI, G. CARETTONI, E. GJERSTAD, and S. M. PUGLISI, 'Nuove indagini in Roma antichissima' in the *Bollettino di Paletnologia Italiana*, LXIV, 1954–5. The authors' respective sections are (1) 'Problemi archeologichi e storici di Roma primitiva', (2) 'Tomba arcaica e cremazione scoperta sul Palatino', (3) 'La stratigrafia e i piu antichi materiali archeologichi nella zona de l'arco di Augusto', (4) 'Sepolcri di incinerati nella valle del Foro romano'.

The question of primitive huts is dealt with in J. DE MORGAN, *L'humanité préhistorique*, Paris, 1921, and that of Italic hut urns in J. SUNDWALL, 'Die italischen Hüttenurnen' in *Acta Academiae Aboensis Humaniora*, IV, 1925. For an attempt to reconstruct the Iron and Bronze Age huts after the model of the hut urns see G. PATRONI, 'Architettura preistorica' in *Storia dell'Architettura*, I, Bergamo, 1951, pp. 35 ff. All the large manuals of Roman history touch on the question of the primitive peoples of Rome. A hypercritical position is taken up by E. PAIS in *Storia di Roma*, Turin, 1898, 2 vols. The thesis by A. PIGANIOL, *Essai sur les origines de Rome*, Paris, 1917, emphasizes the fundamental dualism and the opposition between the Latin and Sabine groups. A general survey of the problems involved is given by E. CIACĘRI in *Le origini di Roma. La monarchia e la prima fase della eta repubblicana*, Milan, 1937.

Two comprehensive studies on the subject of Roman origins have recently appeared: Pietro de Francisci, *Primordia Civitatis,* Rome, 1959; and Hermann Müller-Karpe, *Vom Anfang Roms,* Heidelberg, 1959. Readers should go to the fourth edition (1962) when consulting my own book *Les Origines de Rome,* Coll. *Que sais-je?,* Paris, 1946.

The archaeological bibliography given above will also be of use in connexion with this chapter. For the question of Roman and Latin building techniques, see an excellent book by G. LUGLI, *La tecnica edilizia romana con particolare riguardo a Roma e Lazio,* 2 vols., Rome, 1957. For the period of the Etruscan monarchy see the books on Etruria mentioned above, and also M. PALLOTTINO, *Etruscologia,* 3rd edition, Milan, 1955. The question of the royal walls at Rome has stimulated much discussion and a large number of written works. The attitude of G. SÄFLUND (*Le mura di Roma repubblicana,* Lund, 1932), who denies the existence of any continuous wall before the fourth century, is difficult to defend. For a detailed study and accurate conclusions see TENNEY FRANK, 'Roman Buildings of the Republic' in *Papers and Monographs of the American Academy in Rome,* III, 1924; G. LUGLI, 'Le mura di Servio Tullio e le cosi dette mura serviane', *Historia,* XI, 1933; P. QUONIAM, 'A propos du mur dit de Servius Tullius' in *Mélanges de l'Ecole française de Rome,* LIX, 1947. On the sculptor Vulca and his school, see M. PALLOTTINO, *La scuola di Vulca,* Rome, 1946. For the frescoes of the François Tomb at Vulci a bibliography will be found in the catalogue of the 1955 Etruscan exhibition, *Mostra dell'Arte e della Civiltà etrusca,* Milan, 2nd edition, 1955. See also the study by F. MESSERSCHMIDT, 'Nekropolen von Vulci' in the *Jahrbuch des deutschen Instituts,* 1930. Many works have been published on the subject of the first Greek imports into Etruria and Latium. A systematic bibliography will be found in G. VALLET, *Rhegion et Zancle: Histoire, commerce et civilisation des cités chalcidiennes du détroit de Messine,* Bibliothèque des Ecoles françaises d'Athènes et Rome, 1958.

On the end of the Etruscan period in Rome, see my articles 'Rome de 509 à 475 environ avant J.C.', in the *Revue des Études Latines,* XXXVII, 1959, pp. 118–31; and 'Le départ des Étrusques de Rome et la dédicace du temple de Jupiter capitolin', in the *Revue de l'Histoire des Religions,* 149, April–June 1961, pp. 141–56.

CHAPTER V

CHAPTER VI On account of the scope of these questions the literature dealing with them is extremely ample. The works which follow cover the main elements. The vexed problem of the place of Latin amongst the Indo-European languages is well treated by M. LEJEUNE in 'La position du latin dans le domaine indo-européen' in the *Mémorial des Etudes latines,* Paris, 1943, pp. 7–31.

For the history and structure of the Latin language, see: A. MEILLET, *Esquisse d'une histoire de la langue latine,* Paris, 1928; M. NIEDERMANN, *Précis de phonétique historique du latin,* Paris, 3rd edition, 1953; A. ERNOUT, *Morphologie historique du latin,* Paris, 3rd edition, 1953; A. ERNOUT and F. THOMAS, *Syntaxe latine,* Paris, 2nd edition, 1953; A. ERNOUT and A. MEILLET, *Dictionnaire étymologique de la langue latine,* Paris, 3rd edition, 1951. For the question of the adaption of the Etruscan alphabet in regions outside Etruria, see M. LEJEUNE, 'Notes de linguistique italique, XIII, sur les adaptations de l'alphabet étrusque aux langues indo-européennes d'Italie' in the *Revue des Etudes Latines,* XXXV, 1957.

On the language of Praeneste, see A. ERNOUT, 'Le parler de Préneste d'après les inscriptions' in the *Mémoires de la Société de Linguistique,* XIII, 1905, pp. 233–349. On the Faliscan language, see E. STOLTE, *Der faliskische Dialekt,* Diss., Munich, 1926.

The archaic inscriptions of Rome can be found in the *Corpus Inscriptionum Latinarum,* I, 1st edition by T. MOMMSEN, 1863, 2nd edition by G. HENZEN, C. HUELSEN, and E. LOMMATZSCH, Berlin, 1893–1943.

There is a choice of different studies of the oldest literary and epigraphic texts: A. ERNOUT, *Recueil de textes latins archaïques,* new edition, Paris, 1957; E. H. WARMINGTON, *Vetera latina,* 4 vols., Loeb Edition, London and Cambridge, 1935; A. DEGRASSI, *Inscriptiones latinae liberae rei publicae,* XXIII, in the 'Biblioteca di Studi superiori', Florence, 1957.

The inscription on the *Lapis Niger* is studied by G. DUMÉZIL in 'L'inscription archaïque du Forum et Ciceron, De divinatione', II, p. 36, in *Recherches de Science religieuse,* 1951–2, XXXIX–XL, Mélanges Jules Lebreton, pp. 17 ff. See also M. LEJEUNE, 'A propos de trois inscriptions italiques' in the *Revue des Etudes anciennes,* LIV, 3-4, July–December 1952, p. 340. The site of the *lucus Feroniae* was localized by reference to inscriptions dating from the third century B.C. See R. BLOCH and G. FOTI, 'Nouvelles dédicaces archaïques a la Déesse Feronia' in the *Revue de Philologie,* 1953, I, pp. 65 ff.

The Etruscan influence on Roman onomastics is treated in W. SCHULZE's *Zur Geschichte lateinischer Eigennamen*, Berlin, 1904: Etruscan loan-words in Latin are dealt with by A. ERNOUT in 'Les éléments étrusques du vocabulaire latin', *Bulletin de la Société de Linguistique*, 1930, pp. 82 ff.

An analysis of the Etruscan inscriptions found in Rome has been published by M. PALLOTTINO in 'La iscrizione arcaica su vaso di bucchero rinvenuta ai piedi del Campidoglio', *Bollettino Communale di Roma*, LXIX, 1941, and 'Rivista di epigrafia etrusca' in *Studi Etruschi*, XXII, 1952–3, pp. 309 ff.

For the Etruscan frescoes showing *Phersu*, see G. BECCATI and F. MAGI, 'Le pitture delle tombe degli Auguri e del Pulcinella' in the *Monumenti della Pittura antica scoperti in Italia*, Section I, 'La pittura etrusca, Tarquinii', III–IV, Rome, 1955, and R. BARTOCCINI, C. M. LERICI, and M. MORETTI, *La tomba delle Olimpiadi*, Milan, 1959.

Law and Religion

On the 'sacrum', see E. RHODE, *Psyché*, 2nd edition, Fribourg, 1898; R. CAILLOIS, *L'homme et le sacré*, 'Mythes et Religions' series, Paris, 1939, and W. WARDE FOWLER, *The Religious Experience of the Roman People from the Earliest Times to the Age of Augustus*, London, 1911.

The sociological aspects of religion are analysed by E. DURCKHEIM in *Les formes élémentaires de la vie religieuse*, Paris, 3rd edition, 1937.

Primitive Roman law is studied by H. LÉVY-BRUHL in *Quelques problèmes du très ancien droit romain (essai de solution sociologique)*, Paris, 1934. See also J. CARCOPINO, 'Les prétendues lois royales' in *Mélanges de l'Ecole francaise de Rome*, 1937, pp. 344 ff. and P. F. GIRARD, *Textes de droit romain*, Paris, 5th edition.

Two excellent works of recent date give useful bibliographies for the Roman religion and the problems it presents: A. GRENIER, *Les religions étrusque et romaine*, vol. III of the Collection Mana, Paris, 1944, and J. BAYET, *Histoire politique et psychologique de la religion romaine*, Paris, 1957. Monsieur Bayet's work, which we have found of great assistance in writing this book, lucidly outlines the various facets of Roman religious consciousness and gives a precise account of the principal lines of its complex history.

G. DUMÉZIL's studies in comparative mythology have been mentioned above. For a good working text, see P. GRIMAL, *Dictionnaire de la mythologie grecque et romaine*, Paris, 1951.

On the magical aspects of the Roman religion, see SIR JAMES FRAZER, *The Golden Bough*, London, 1890, and more recently, H. WAGENVOORT, *Roman Dynamism*, Oxford, 1947.

On divination, see A. BOUCHÉ-LECLERCQ, *Histoire de la divination dans l'Antiquité*, 4 vols., Paris, 1879–88. On omens, see R. BLOCH, *Les prodiges dans l'Antiquité classique (Grèce, Étrurie et Rome)*, in the series 'Mythes et Religions', Paris, 1962.

The significance of the games is analysed by A. PIGANIOL in *Recherches sur les jeux romains*, Strasbourg, 1923. The Salians' dances have been treated in two recent articles: R. BLOCH, 'Une tombe villanovienne près de Bolsena et la danse guerrière dans l'Italie primitive' in *Mélanges de l'Ecole Française*, 1958, and 'Sur les danses armées des Saliens' in *Annales, Economies-Sociétés-Civilisations*, 1958, 3rd volume. On the 'evocatio' see V. BASANOFF's *Evocatio, Etude d'un rituel militaire romain*, Paris, 1947.

Many works have been devoted to the subject of the Roman gods. We will quote only: J. BAYET, *Les origines de l'Hercule romain*, Paris, 1926; A. BRUHL, *Liber Pater, Origine et expansion du culte dionysiaque dans le monde romain*, Paris, 1953; R. SCHILLING, *La religion romaine de Vénus depuis les origines jusqu'au temps d'Auguste*, Paris, 1954; J. GAGÉ, *Apollon romain, Essai sur le culte d'Apollon et le développement du ritus graecus à Rome, des origines à Auguste*, Paris, 1955; A. T. ROSE, *Some problems of classical Religion*, Oslo, 1958. For agrarian cults in Rome, see H. LE BONNIEC, *Le culte de Cérès à Rome, des origines à la fin de la République*, Paris, Klincksieck, 1958; I do not share the author's opinions about the formation of the Ceres-Liber-Libera triad in Rome.

Both private and public religion are treated in the general books on Roman religion and history. It is still worth reading the classic work on the subject, FUSTEL DE COULANGES, *La Cité Antique*, Paris, 1865.

On the death-cult and its importance, see P. JACOBSEN, *Les Mânes*, 3 volumes, Paris, 1924, and in particular, F. CUMONT, *Lux Perpetua*, Paris, 1949.

Glossary

Aediles Curules. Two representatives of the whole people entrusted with temples, other public buildings, corn supplies and games. An office instituted 367 B.C. They were entitled to the *sella curulis* or folding ivory chair, a mark of distinction accorded to high magistrates. The plebeian aediles, instituted in 493 B.C., were guardians of the temple of Ceres, where the *plebiscita* (decrees of the people) were kept.

Bucchero. Fine black pottery—the colour caused by complete reduction during firing—wheel-thrown often with incised or relief decoration. Dates from the seventh to the fifth century B.C. Later forms are clearly influenced by Greek designs.

Capreoli. Short pieces of timber for roof supports.

Cella. Originally meaning a little room or store-room (from *celare*, to hide), this term came to be applied to the walled inner structure of a temple.

Centuria. Term originally applied to a unit in the military organization of early Rome, which was subsequently incorporated in the electoral systems attributed to Servius Tullius. This allowed for six property classes comprising 193 *centuriae*, each *centuria* being entitled to one vote in the *comitia centuriata* (*q.v.*).

Cippus. A low pillar used as a tombstone or for such purposes as marking boundaries.

Circus Maximus. Situated in the *Vallis Murcia* between the Palatine and Aventine hills, it was founded, according to tradition, by the Tarquins. Its history is complex. See, on this subject, G. Lugli, *Roma antica*, Rome, 1946, pp. 599 f.

Cloaca Maxima. The 'great sewer' running from the Subura valley to drain the marsh at the foot of the Capitol, thus allowing the construction of the Forum. Ascribed to the Tarquins, it certainly dates from Etruscan times. It was reconstructed by Augustus and indeed still forms part of the municipal drainage system.

Comitia centuriata. The assembly of the *centuriae* (*q.v.*).

Comitium. A paved area 80 yds square on the north-west side of the

Forum used for the meetings of the *comitia*. To the north lay the *Curia* (*q.v.*), and to the south the *Rostra* (*q.v.*).

Consualia. Festivals held on 15 December and 21 August associated with Consus, a deity concerned with agriculture and the Underworld and thus equated with Poseidon. He had an underground altar dedicated to him in the *Circus Maximus* where horse and chariot races were held in his honour. It was during the *Consualia* that the rape of the Sabines took place.

Curia. Senate House. It stood on the north side of the *Comitium* (*q.v.*), and was ascribed to Tullus Hostilius.

Dolium. A large bell-mouthed storage-jar frequently used as a coffin.

Eques. A 'Horseman' or 'Knight'. The *equites* were the cavalry and in the early military system were the wealthiest members of the *comitia centuriata* (*q.v.*), in which they formed 18 *centuriae* (*q.v.*).

Fasces. The bundle of rods enclosing the axe carried by the lictors before senior magistrates, usually made out of birch.

Feriae Latinae. The great common festival of the early Latin communities, held on the Alban Mount.

Fetialis. One of 20 men elected for life for maintenance of the laws concerning international relations. They were apparently attached to the temple of Jupiter Feretrius.

Flamen. One of 15 priests of the gods of the old order. Chief amongst them were the priests of Jupiter, Mars, and Quirinus, all being patricians. They were exempted from military service and taxation and in general from taking political office.

Fossa. The typical trench-grave of the pre-Etruscan cultures, containing as a rule extended inhumation burials and also, on occasion, cremations.

Hoplites. Greek term for heavy armed infantry.

Hydria. A large two- or three-handled jar employed for carrying or storing liquids.

Impasto. The typical poorer quality local ware formed mostly by roughly shaping by hand and finished on a wheel. The blackish-brown or red colouring was due to the poor firing of the red clay. The pots were often burnished and incised or impressed mainly with geometric patterns. The forms were of a great variety.

Kantharos. High-handled drinking cup, a Greek form adopted by native Italian potters in the *bucchero* style (*q.v.*).

Lucumon. Term applied to Etruscan aristocrats and in particular to the chiefs who ruled over each town.

Lupercalia. Festival of purification held on 15 February at the Lupercal, the cave on the Palatine where Romulus and Remus were supposed to have been suckled by the wolf.

Numen. The power or spirit in each natural object, extended to that force controlling the nature and the actions of man. The word derives from the verb *nuere*, to nod.

Oinochoe. Beaked wine flagon.

Olla. A pot-shaped jar with lid.

Princeps. Courtesy title given to the leading individual in a public body, and adopted in the Imperial period by Augustus and his successors.

Rostra. Literally the beaks and originally the prows of ships set up on the orators' platform in the Forum following the capture *c.* 340 B.C. of the Volscian fleet off Antium.

Sacrarium (*Ancilia condere*). The repository for the *ancilia* or sacred shields on the Palatine.

Sepolcreto. The pre-Etruscan cemetery beneath the Forum extending from a point south-east of the temple of Faustina first discovered in 1902.

Suovetaurilia. The sacrifice of pigs, sheep and bulls, performed as a special measure to obtain the favour of the gods.

Terremare. The extensive prehistoric settlements of the Po valley occupied from Early Bronze Age times.

Toga palmata. The decorated toga worn by the *triumphator* (*q.v.*).

Toga praetexta. Purple-bordered toga worn by free-born youths, magistrates and those concerned with religious rites.

Triumphator. 'The triumphing one', the victorious leader, was accustomed to drive in a chariot preceded by the whole Senate, then by the spoils of battle including prisoners. With him in the chariot rode a slave as a reminder of the transitoriness of success. The chariot was followed by the victorious army. The procession proceeded along the Via Sacra to the Capitol where sacrifice was offered to Jupiter Feretrius.

Vallis Murcia see *Circus Maximus.*

Sources of Illustrations

Pl. 1 and 2: Rotalfoto, Milan; pl. 4: Anderson; pl. 3, 6, 7, 48, 49, 52, 53, 60: Franceschi, Paris; pl. 8 and 9: from *L'Ara Pacis Augustae* by G. Moretti, Rome, 1948; pl. 5: Atterocca, Terni; pl. 55: *Paris-Match*; pl. 54–7: Silvana, Milan.

The other photographs were provided through the courtesy of various scholars for whose generosity and willing co-operation I am most grateful. Pl. 10 and 11 are from the photographic archives of the Vatican Museum, whose Directors are Professori Josi, De Campos and Magi; pl. 58 is from the photographic section of the Department of Antiquities of Southern Etruria (Director: Professore Bartoccini); pl. 59 is from the photographic section of the Department of Antiquities of Central and Northern Etruria (Director: Professore Caputo); pl. 12–14, 21–46, 50, 51, are from the photographic section of the Department of Antiquities of the Forum and Palatine (Director: Professore P. Romanelli); pl. 15–18 are from the photographic section of the Italian Ministry of Education; pl. 20 is from a photograph by Miss Georgina Masson.

I acknowledge, with profound gratitude, the help given me by Mlle Speyer, Professori Josi, Magi, Bartoccini, Caputo, Romanelli, Foti and Maetzke. I also tender my grateful thanks to my old friends, Dottoressa Floriani Squarciapino and Dottore G. F. Carettoni.

2

3

4

5

6

7

8

11

12

13

14

19

20

21

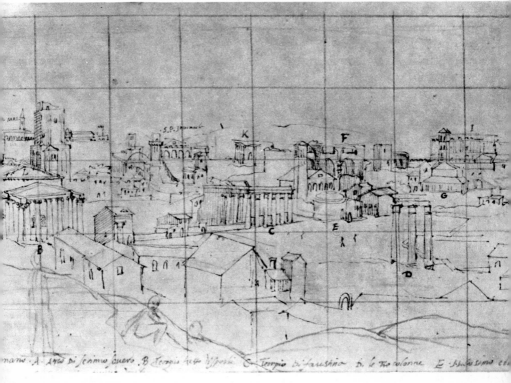

22

23

24

26

27

8

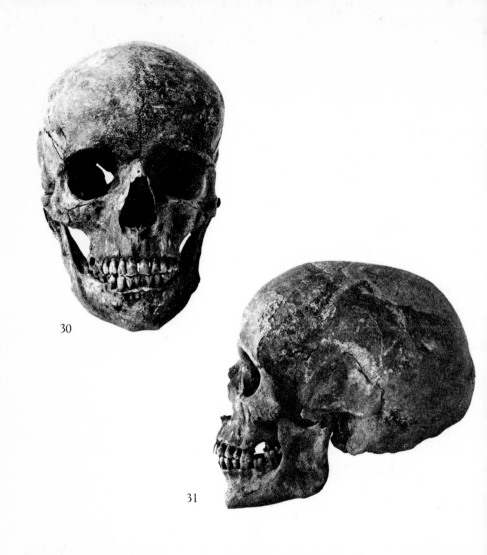

30

31

32

33

34

35

36

37

38

39

40

41

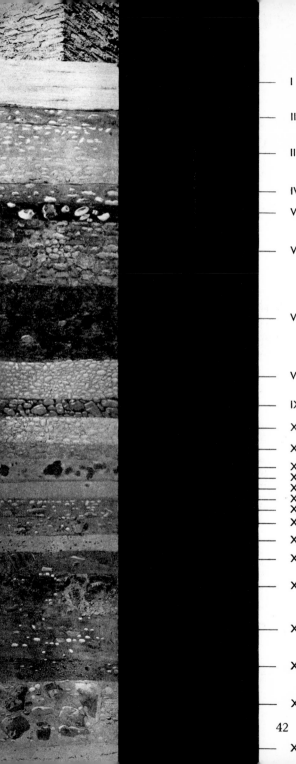

I

II

III

IV

V

VI

VII

VIII

IX

X

XI

XII
XIII
XIV
XV
XVI
XVII

XVIII

XIX

XX

XXI

XXII

XXIII

42

XXIV

43

45

44

46

47

48

49

50

51

52

53

56

58

59

MVNIFICENTIA · PII · SEXTI · P · M

Notes on the Plates

1, 2 Two warriors: small Sardinian bronzes. In pre-Roman Sardinia there grew up a form of small-scale bronze sculpture consisting of characteristic figurines, of which 400 survive today; a large number of these are exhibited in the Museum of Cagliari. The bronzes have much in common with sculpture of the protohistorical Mediterranean world and may be associated with the figurines of Luristan, Armenia, Syria, Asia Minor, Greece, and Spain. The oriental influences discernible in these small, stylized and almost filiform Sardinian bronzes may have been brought into the country by Phoenician trade and trading-posts in Sardinia. But it is equally probable that they were due to the influence of the art of Etruria, a country so much nearer. The date of this group is hard to establish: it is probably from the seventh or sixth century B.C. cf. M. Pallottino, *La Sardegna nuragica,* Rome, 1950. Height (1) $7\frac{1}{16}$ in., (2) $5\frac{7}{8}$ in. In the Museum at Cagliari.

3 Aeneas and Anchises. Small terracotta group from Veii, probably a copy of a larger statue. cf. the catalogue of the *Mostra dell'Arte e della Civiltà etrusca,* 2nd edition, Milan, 1955, no. 273. First half of the fifth century B.C. 6 ft. high. Museum of the Villa Giulia, Rome.

4 The Warrior of Capestrano. The warrior is shown with his arms, parts of a cuirass and a huge helmet topped with a tall crest. The helmet is 1 ft. 3 in. high, with a diameter of 2 ft. $1\frac{5}{8}$ in. The face is covered by a mask. On one of the supports is a pre-Sabellian inscription containing forty letters.

The shape of the body, with the excessive development of the shoulders and hips and very slim waist, gives the work a strange and primitive appearance. It is an exceptional example of an ancient form of Italic statuary which had been influenced by sixth-century Greek sculpture and responded with a rough, brutal style. The mask is probably of a funerary character, but it could also be a ceremonial object. The work probably dates from the sixth century. Near the site of the find excavations have in fact revealed thirty-three inhumation graves of which twenty-one date from the end of the seventh and the sixth centuries. The Warrior of Capestrano has been the subject of numerous studies, often with different conclusions. However, its essential characteristics—the mouth with tightly closed lips, the eyes surrounded by raised rims, the heavily accented curves, the geometrization of the lines—are common in many artistic productions of the pre- or sub-classical Mediterranean world (from Mesopotamia to Sardinia). The enormous helmet is no doubt of Illyrian origin. Macedonians and Illyrians did in fact wear hats with very broad brims. The inscription, the interpretation of which presents serious difficulties, no doubt indicates the name and family of the deceased. cf. G. Moretti, 'Il guerriero italico di Capestrano' in *Opere d'Arte*, VI, 1936, the epigraphical appendix by F. Ribezzo, and A. Boethius's comments in *Die Antike*, XVI, pp. 177 sqq., 1940. See also pp. 1 sqq. in S. Ferri's 'Osservazioni intorno al guerriero di Capestrano' in the *Bollettino d'Arte*, XXIV, 1949, and M. Pallottino's 'Capestranezze' in *Archeologia Classica*, I, 1949, pp. 208 sqq.

There is an interesting hypothesis which seeks to account for this strange stone statue by reference to the rite of the *devotio* which we have analysed above (p. 132 sq.) and which was probably practised not only by the Latins but also by other peoples of ancient Italy. It will be remembered that, if the legionary to be 'sacrificed' by his general was not killed in battle, one had to bury a statue at least 7 ft. tall. Now, the height of the warrior of Capestrano is 6 ft. 9½ in., that is, roughly seven Roman feet. It has therefore been suggested that the statue is of a *devotus* who escaped death. I am personally much tempted by an explanation of this kind. If it is correct, the mask may well have been used as a ceremonial accessory by the *devotus* at the moment when he charged the enemy, and destined to increase their shock and sacred terror. For this interpretation of the mask, cf. my section on 'Etruria and the Roman World' in the catalogue of the exhibition of masks held in the Musée Guimet, Paris, in 1959. For the theory that the warrior was a *devotus,* cf. Louise Adams Holland, 'The Purpose of the Warrior Image from Capestrano' in the *American Journal of Archaeology*, LX, 1956, and A. Boethius, 'Livy, VIII, 10, 12, and the warrior image from Capestrano' in *Eranos*, LIV, 1957. Nevertheless the presence of a female bust, which was found at the same time as the male statue, creates added difficulties.

Notes on the Plates

5 She-wolf from the Capitol. Large bronze, probably of the school of Veii and dating from about 500 B.C. Height 2 ft. 9½ in. The twins are a Renaissance addition. Palazzo dei Conservatori, Rome.

6 Bas-relief decorating the bottom of an Etruscan funerary stele from Bologna: she-wolf suckling a child. It is impossible to say whether this is in fact an allusion to the Roman legend. The stele is 4 ft. tall and dates from the first half of the fourth century B.C. Museum of Bologna.

7 Silver coin from Rome, showing the she-wolf suckling the twins. This coin, in a lively Hellenistic style, is only a little earlier than the first Punic War and dates from 269 B.C. The word *Romano* is in fact the ancient genitive plural of *Romanus* from which the final *m* has dis-appeared. The ancient ending for this case was *ōm*, which developed into *um*. The Classical Latin *orum* was formed on analogy with the *arum* ending of the first declension.

8 Aeneas sacrificing to the Penates. The *Ara Pacis* now stands once again on the Campus Martius near the Tiber, for it has been possible to make a very successful reconstruction of it. The inside and outside walls of the enclosure are decorated with bas-reliefs and the faces of the west door show two scenes recalling Rome's earliest origins: Aeneas sacrificing to the Penates and the she-wolf suckling the twins in the Lupercal. Only small fragments of the latter survive, but the other panel, probably the finest portion of the whole monument, is well preserved.

Aeneas is shown here as a bearded figure with noble and austere features; his head is covered with a cloak and his chest bare. He is offering up a sacrifice to the Penates on a rustic altar. This scene is a splendid illustration of Roman 'piety', which under Augustus became one of the most important themes in both literature and art.

After G. Moretti's monumental work, *Ara Pacis Augustae,* 2 vols., in fol., Rome, 1948.

9 Figure of Aeneas. (Detail of pl. 8.)

10, 11 Heads of the god, Mars, and the goddess, Rome, in the bas-reliefs of the Cancellaria. These two sculpted panels, each 19 ft. 8 in. wide, show an arrival (*adventus*) of the Emperor Vespasian, and a departure (*profectio;* but some think this is in fact another scene of an arrival at the *Urbs*) of his son Domitian. After Domitian's *damnatio memoriae* his head was trans-formed into a head of Nerva. The bas-reliefs as a whole were to decorate the attic of a triumphal arch and were executed about 83–5 ·on the orders of Domitian, after his great victory over the Parthians. The work is harmoniously composed but has a certain academic coldness. cf. F. Magi, *I rilievi Flavi del Palazzo della Cancellaria*, Rome, 1946. Vatican Museum.

12,13,14   Bas-reliefs of the Basilica Aemilia. Sculpted on marble slabs 2 ft. 5⅛ in. high. A slight extension of the lower part of these slabs forms a kind of base, on which the figures stand. The frieze depicted various episodes in the legend of the origins of Rome. Pl. 12 shows the punishment of Tarpeia—the only surviving monumental representation of this subject. In front of a bearded man who is probably Titus Tatius, soldiers crush Tarpeia beneath the weight of their shields. Tarpeia, with extended arms, is almost hidden beneath the weapons. cf. G. C. Picard, *Les Trophées Romains*, Paris, 1957, p. 108. Pl. 13 shows a very beautiful but unfortunately disfigured relief representing the building of an enclosure wall, using the technique of the *opera quadrata*. We know from the surviving portions of Servius's walls at Rome that they used this building technique. The scene shown represents the building of the wall either of Alba or of Rome itself; the animated scene shown in pl. 14 is that of the rape of the Sabines. While the whole frieze, neo-Classical art but in a style very different from that of the *Ara Pacis*, probably dates from the end of the Republic or the beginning of the Empire, as in many other works of the same period it was to exalt the founders and origins of the *Urbs*. cf. A. Bartoli, 'Il fregio figurato della Basilica Aemilia', *Bollettino d'Arte*, XXXV, pp. 289 sqq.

15, 16   Hut foundations on the Palatine.

17, 18   Model reconstruction of the hut whose plan is shown in pl. 16. Antiquarium of the Palatine.

19   The Tiber Island.

20   View of the Forum, Rome. Left: the temple of Antoninus and Faustina.

21   The series of monuments below the *Lapis Niger*. Drawn by the architect Cirilli. Excavation of 1900.

22   The Forum Romanum in the sixteenth century. Drawn by G. Antonio Dosio (Florence).

23   The cemetery of the Forum, at the beginning of Boni's excavations.

24   The floor of the Forum cemetery during the excavations.

25   The Forum cemetery, after the excavations were completed.

26   Model of the cemetery of the Forum. Antiquarium of the Forum.

27   Repaired floor of the cemetery after the end of the excavations.

28   Cemetery of the Forum: grave B at the time it was uncovered. cf. *Notizie degli Scavi*, 1903, p. 128.

29   Inhumation grave B. cf. *Notizie degli Scavi*, 1906, p. 253, and E. Gjerstad, *Early Rome—II: The Tombs*, pp. 19 sqq. The dimensions of the grave are: length 9 ft. 8⅛ in., depth 5 ft. 3¾ in., maximum width 3 ft. 1⅜ in. It was covered and surrounded by stones. The longitudinal axis ran N.E.–S.W. The body buried was that of an adult about 5 ft. 4 in. tall, and the skeleton, lying on its back, is well preserved. Near the skull the bones of a young pig offered as a sacrifice have been found, as well as several grains of corn. On the left part of the thorax was placed a bronze fibula *ad arco serpeggiante*; arranged round the head were a cup with two handles, a cup with one handle and an *impasto* bowl, all hand-made; at the feet, a bowl and globular amphora of the same material. The grave dates from a little later than the middle of the eighth century.

30, 31   Skull of the skeleton from grave B.

32   An excellent reconstruction of grave B in the Antiquarium of the Forum.

33   Material from grave Q (omitting a bobbin for weaving, fragments of bronze rings and pieces of amber). In the centre, the hut urn, 9½ in. tall,

1 ft. ⅝ in. long, 11⅜ in. broad. It contained burned bones, probably those of a young woman and fragments of bronze and amber. On the human bones were three unburned turtle-dove's bones. Arranged around the hut urn were bowls with reticulated decoration, bowls with handles, cups, a lid; all these receptacles being in a hand-made *impasto*. The date of the tomb is a little later than the middle of the eighth century.

34 Inhumation grave P, while being excavated. cf. *Notizie degli Scavi*, 1905, p. 183, and E. Gjerstad, *op. cit.*, p. 101.

35 Cremation grave Q. cf. *Notizie degli Scavi*, 1906, p. 10, and Gjerstad, *op. cit.*, p. 26. This is a *pozzo*-grave, diameter 3 ft. 5⅜ in., average depth 4 ft. 5⅛ in. At the bottom of the *pozzo* is the place where the ashes were actually deposited: 2 ft. 5⅛ in. long, 1 ft. 10 in. wide, and 1 ft. 1¾ in. deep. The material shown in the photograph was covered by eight pieces of tufa and the *pozzo* itself was filled with earth and pieces of tufa.

36 Inhumation grave P when the stones and covering had been removed. The *fossa* is 5 ft. 10⅞ in. long, 3 ft. 1⅜ in. deep, and 2 ft. 11⅜ in. wide. The longitudinal axis runs N.W.–S.E. The grave contains the bones of a child six to eight years old: on the thorax had been placed a fibula *ad arco serpeggiante*, at the head and feet vases for offerings (*impasto* vases handworked).

37 Reconstruction of grave P in the Antiquarium of the Forum. The grave dates from the second half of the eighth century B.C.

38 Grave I: coffin made of a scooped-out oak trunk and containing the remains of a girl of about two. cf. *Notizie degli Scavi*, 1903, p. 398, and E. Gjerstad, *op. cit.*, p. 125. On the skelton were found two fibulae *a navicella*, an ivory bracelet, and the remains of a necklace of paste.

39 Vases discovered by Boni inside a block of travertine forming part of the base of the Equus Domitiani on the Forum. cf. E. Gjerstad, *Early Rome—I*, p. 82. The amphora and the two kyathoi with incised decoration are of Faliscan make. The whole dates from the second quarter of the seventh century. In E. Gjerstad's view it is in fact material from a child's grave situated beside one of the huts which then occupied the area, and

discovered during the building of the bases for the *Equus Domitiani*. As Roman law forbade interference with a grave (unless the Pontiffs decided otherwise) the material in the grave discovered was left where it was but used as a propitiatory offering in the building then being undertaken.

40 Proto-Corinthian ovoid *aryballos,* part of the material from *fossa*-grave G, cf. fig. 14. It dates from about 650 B.C. and offers reliable evidence as to date. Grave G is one of the latest in the Roman Forum. cf. *Notizie degli Scavi,* 1903, p. 388 and E. Gjerstad, II, p. 125.

41 Reconstruction of grave I in the Antiquarium of the Forum. Beside the coffin, wheel-made votive vases, among which is a *skyphos* of bucheroid *impasto* and two Italo-Corinthian *skyphoi*. One vase contained the bones of a fish. The grave (described as a *feretro*) dates from the second quarter of the seventh century.

42 Section showing the stratigraphy of Boni's excavations in the centre of the *Comitium.* The following layers are worthy of comment:

   (I)   Medieval pavement incorporating material of up to the eleventh century A.D.

   (II) Soil indicating level of pavement at the end of the Empire and fourth-century A.D. pedestal foundations.

   (IV) Earth foundation level of the first pavement of the imperial period.

   (V) Layer containing the structures beneath the *Lapis Niger* (pl. XXI), remains of sacrifices, and sherds of Chalcidean 'black figure' ware.

   (VI) Tufa foundation of the latest Republican pavement level.

   (VII) Earth layer showing evidence of burning, ritual pits, and four levels of paving in *opus signinum*. Italo-Corinthian ware, clay figurines in the Archaic style, and sherds of *impasto*.

   (IX) Tufa containing fragment of terra-cotta antefix illustrated in fig. 16.

   (XVII) Layer of earth and gravel containing black *bucchero* sherds.

(xix)   Clayey layer containing a mass of roofing tiles and sherds of seventh-century B.C. Rhodian ware.

(xxiii) Lowest occupation level of blackish earth permeated with gravel and including fragments of a jar of Villanovan type.

(xix)   Yellowish sandy clay marking the first of the purely geological strata. From the surface of the medieval pavement to the top of this level the section measures 4.48 m. in depth.

(After G. Boni in *Notizie degli scavi di antichita . . . Anno 1900* (1900), p. 318, fig. 18.)

43   Terracotta architectonic fragment discovered by Boni on the site of the *Lapis Niger*. This bas-relief with its accentuated linearism, is one of the decorative terracottas said to belong to the first (or Ionic) phase and dates from the first decades of the sixth century. cf. *Notizie degli Scavi*, 1899, p. 156, fig. 17; and A. Andren, *Architectural Terracottas from Etrusco-Italic Temples,* Lund, Leipzig, 1940, pl. 105. Antiquarium of the Forum.

44   Architectonic frieze of the first phase. First decades of the sixth century. It was discovered on the site of the Arch of Augustus and represents a minotaur walking between two felines. Height $7\frac{7}{8}$ in.; length 1 ft. 3 in. cf. P. Romanelli, 'Terracotte architettoniche del Foro romano' in the *Bollettino d'Arte,* XL, 1955, pp. 203 sqq.

45   Architectonic frieze of the first phase, showing warriors and aurigae on chariots drawn by winged horses. The panel, $9\frac{1}{2}$ in. tall by 1 ft. $11\frac{1}{4}$ in. wide, is of the same type as those found at Velletri. cf. G. Q. Giglioli, *L'arte etrusca,* Milan, 1937, pl. XCVIII, 2 and 3, and pl. C, 2. It was found on the Esquiline and is now in the *Antiquarium Communale, Rome.*

46, 47   Fragment of a terracotta statue showing a warrior. Perhaps originally the acroterium of a temple. This Etruscan work in an Ionian style was found near Sant'Omobono and dates from the last decades of the sixth century. Height 1 ft. $5\frac{3}{8}$ in. cf. the catalogue of the *Mostra dell'Arte e della Civiltà etrusca,* Milan, 2nd edition, 1955, no. 283. *Antiquarium Communale, Rome.*

48, 49 Head of a bearded deity which was probably part of the acroterium placed on the top of the temple of the Mater Matuta à Satricum. This Etrusco-Latin work in a belated archaic style reveals the hand of an excellent artist. cf. the aforementioned catalogue to the *Mostra Etrusca*, no. 293.

50 Antefix in the form of a head of a maenad, diademed and with an archaic smile. It comes from the *Aracoeli* and decorated one of the temples of the *Arx Capitolina*. Date: *c.* 500 B.C. cf. G. Q. Giglioli, *op. cit.*, pl. CLXXXIII, 3. Palazzo dei Conservatori.

51 Very beautiful antefix in the form of a head of Silenus from Rome. About 550 B.C. cf. G. Q. Giglioli, *op. cit.*, pl. CLXX, II, 4. *Antiquarium Communale, Rome.*

52 Etrusco-Latin terracotta antefix representing a female face surrounded by a richly decorated shell. This work, which comes from the Latin town of Lanuvium, dates from the beginning of the fifth century B.C. In an Ionic-Etruscan style, it has a pleasant, and, as it were, provincial charm. Height 1 ft. 3¾ in. cf. the aforementioned catalogue to the *Mostra Etrusca*, no. 290.

53 Small *bucchero* plate with an engraved Etruscan inscription which reads: 'ni araziia laraniia'. Found on the Capitol. cf. M. Pallottino, *Testimonia linguae etruscae*, Florence, 1954, no. 24.

54 Fresco from the François Tomb at Vulci. Caile Vipinas, who is holding out his chained hands, is being freed by someone called Mastarna. The date of these frescoes is variously given as the beginning and end of the Hellenistic period. cf. M. Pallottino, *La Peinture Etrusque*, Skira, 1952, pp. 115 sqq. Torlonia Museum, Rome.

55 Part of the Piazza Bocca della Verità which is on the site of the ancient Forum Boarium. In its present form the round temple, commonly called the Temple of Vesta, is a copy from the Augustan period. The purpose for which it was intended remains an enigma. cf. G. Lugli, *Roma Antica, il centro monumentale*, Rome, 1946, pp. 579 sqq.

56   Podium and colonnade of the Temple of Saturn on the north-west side of the Forum. It was often restored, the last time being in the fourth century, A.D. The six front columns are of grey granite, the two side columns of red granite: they are 36 ft. 1⅛ in. tall. The temple contained the *aerarium populi romani,* also called the *aerarium Saturni.* cf. G. Lugli, *op. cit.,* p. 149.

57   Fresco from the Tomb of the Augurs. A masked person, *Phersu,* racing or fleeing: Tarquinia, 530 B.C. cf. G. Beccati and F. Magi, *Le Pitture delle Tombe degli Auguri e del Pulcinella,* in the series *Monumenti della Pittura Antica Scoperti in Italia,* Rome, 1955.

58   Biconical bronze vase found in the cemetery of Bisenzio. On the shoulder of the lid is a magical scene showing an armed dance. Height 9⅞ in. The vase dates from the first quarter of the seventh century B.C. Museum of the Villa Giulia, Rome.

59   Agate intaglio in the Archaeological Museum of Florence, showing 'the moving of the *ancilia*' by two Salian priests. The photograph has been greatly enlarged: in fact the gem measures ¾ in. by ¹⁹⁄₃₂ in. cf. A. Furt-wängler, *Die Antiken Gemmen,* Leipzig, 1900, pl. XXII, 64, and G. Q. Giglioli, 'Due monumente inediti del Museo Lateranense, La Processione dei Salii' in the *Rendiconti della Pontificia Accademia romana di archeologia,* series III, XXV–XXVI, 1949–51, pp. 95 sqq. Hellenistic period. The inscription: 'Appius alce', meaning 'Appius gave', links a Latin name with an Etruscan verb. cf. M. Pallottino, *Testimonia linguae etruscae,* no. 777.

60   Statue of Juno Sospita from Lanuvium. The goddess is advancing into battle. She wears a goatskin, brandishes a lance with her right hand, and with her left holds her *scutulum.* Sala Rotonda, Vatican Museum.

Index